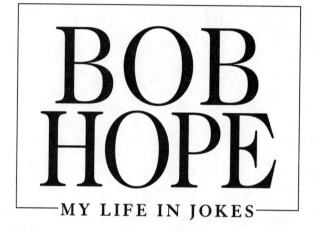

BOB HOPE
MY LIFE IN JOKES

BY BOB HOPE
with Linda Hope

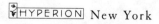 New York

For more information, please visit www.bobhope.com

*To all the audiences, military and civilian, who have
sustained me for a century with their laughter.
To my writers, who put the words in my mouth.
And most especially, to Dolores, without whose love,
sacrifice, golf game, and humor my life would
not have been possible.*

CONTENTS

INTRODUCTION

IT'S HARD TO BELIEVE that my dad is going to be celebrating his 100th birthday on May 29, 2003. Looking back at his life has been an awesome experience. So much history, so many jokes!

I am struck by the fact that Dad's development parallels the growth and development of our country. When he was born, electricity was hardly a household word. Henry Ford established the Ford Motor Company a hundred years ago, and 1903 was the year the Wright Brothers took their first flight. So many of the cornerstones of our current way of life were born when Bob Hope was.

From the '30s on, he began to look at his surroundings and comment on what was happening in a humorous way. These observations, his jokes, have given us a way of looking at the world from a different perspective. Because his material was always topical, it was, in a way, like a developing news story. He had no idea of how the person or event would turn out. He was simply taking a funny snapshot, freezing a moment in time. He took our pulse as a country and told us how we were feeling.

When I started this project, I was immediately impressed by the enormity of it. I had written and produced the A&E biography on my dad, so I felt like I had a bit of a leg up when I decided to tackle this book. But this was a much different kind of job, and in many ways a more personal one. It allowed me to look at his life, his life's work, and his reaction to both. By reading all of his own accounts of his life, I got to see how he perceived things. I was, in many cases, then able to match them up with what I witnessed in all those years growing up and working with him.

When I went through his joke files, I got such a kick out of finding handwritten jokes on the backs of envelopes and paper napkins. It made me feel almost like I was there. To come upon some of his old vaudeville jokes in his writing on yellowed and tattered paper meant so much to me. I combed through thousands of pages of jokes and listened to hours of his transcribed interviews as he told stories of his life. What a life it was!

As I read, I was struck with the businesslike way he approached his jokes. He loved words and enjoyed the process of finding the best way to arrange them so they were funny. As any of his writers can tell you, he was a master editor. He always tried to get the best out of the writers and would often pit them against each other to see who could come up with the wittiest material. Sometimes he would take part of one joke and combine it with part of another, or write or rewrite a punch line. Mostly, he enjoyed getting up in front of an audience and trying out new routines, loving the laughter when things worked and working hard to "save" jokes that died. Dad loved what he did.

I like to think that all of the laughter he evoked in all of his audiences, military or civilian, those dressed in black tie or those enjoying him at a State Fair, all of those laughs are out there somewhere, bringing him joy and comfort in his old age.

It's been a great privilege to be a part of his life, to have worked for him and with him for the last twenty-five years. I have learned so much from him as a father: the value of hard work, responsibility to others, and above all, the importance of sharing laughter. Thank you, Dad, for all the memories.

—Linda Hope

NOTE TO THE READER

THE USUAL DISCLAIMER contains language like "The names have been changed to protect the innocent." Well, in this case, the innocent (family, friends) have often been changed to protect the joke. So, forgive and enjoy!

I WAS BORN IN 1903 at Eltham in England. Eltham is about ten miles from London's Charing Cross Station. It's pronounced without the "h." I'll start with my mother, Avis Townes Hope. After all, that's where most people start. What a job she did with her seven rockhead sons. She was so great.

England was the scene of my greatest performance . . . I was born there.

It was a typically British birth . . . I was three at the time . . . They had a strike in the maternity ward . . . I came out in sympathy.

I was destined to be an actor. The day I was born I stood up and took a bow. Really. When the doctor slapped me, I thought it was applause.

It was probably a coincidence, but right after I was born, my mom and dad left town.

My folks were English . . . we were too poor to be British.

I don't know who was king then, but they didn't hold it against him.

Of course, the king was smart . . . he blamed it on the previous administration.

England is where my roots are . . . and let me tell you, I've got more roots than a reformed punk rocker.

I was able to find my original birth certificate, but it took three guys to help me get it. Stone tablets are heavy.

My old house in Eltham is still standing. They even put a little plaque on the outside . . . "Last bathroom before Scotland."

In England, I was the youngest of five boys. After they had me, Mum and Daddy never spoke to each other again.

I was Mom's favorite, though. She was always playing with me and tossing me in the air . . . What fun it would have been if one day she would've caught me.

There were so many in my family, I was eight years old before it was my turn in the bathroom.

In all there were seven brothers. That's how I learned to dance . . . waiting for my turn in the bathroom.

We had the only bathroom in the neighborhood with a revolving door.

I wore hand-me-downs all my life. By the time the trousers got to me, they were so worn that I could sit on a dime and tell you if it was heads or tails.

And by the time my younger brother got them, he could do the same thing sitting on a dollar bill.

The seat of the trousers got so shiny, we'd hang them on the bedpost and they'd double as a night-light.

In those days, shoes were a status symbol!

I came from a very big family. Four of us slept in the same bed. When we got cold, Mother threw on another brother.

With so many boys, my father bought us a dachshund so we could all pet him at the same time.

Though I was born in England, I left at the age of four ... Actually, the minute I started to talk, they deported me.

It was my first command performance.

I left England at an early age, as soon as I was old enough to realize they already had a king.

I CAME OVER TO the United States to start from scratch. It was a scratchy start, all right. In March 1908, when we small Hopes came up out of steerage at Ellis Island, each of us wore two suits of sandpapery underwear under two suits of clothing to save luggage space.

And they tell me I looked adorable getting off the boat . . . clutching my teddy bear and my deportation papers.

I'm half British, half American. My passport has an eagle with a tea bag in its beak.

I'll never forget our first view of the Statue of Liberty carrying her flaming torch on high. Dad turned to me and said, "This is what I've dreamed of, son. A country where women carry their own matches."

In fact, the trip to America is what made me a comedian. My folks forgot to punch air holes in the suitcase.

We moved to Cleveland. Here people lived on the right side of the tracks or the wrong side of the tracks. We lived under the tracks.

———

Looking back at my Cleveland boyhood, I know now that it was grim going. But nobody told us Hopes it was grim. We just thought that's the way things were. We had fun with what we had. We ate regularly, although sometimes when we'd eaten everything on the table, we sat there staring hungrily at each other.

We didn't live it up, but we lived breezy and we had our share of laughs.

———

My mother was a wonderful woman. We were kind of poor and she hated to spend a nickel on herself, so she bought most of her things in a war-surplus store. She was the only woman in Cleveland wearing khaki lipstick.

My mother had so much work to do that when one of us was being born she never used to go to the hospital until the last possible second. In fact, three of us were born on a bus . . . and after each one, Dad would go up and ask for a transfer.

She patched up all our clothes and I got all the hand-me-downs . . . My shirt was so worn and tattered that everyone thought I was wearing a lace shawl.

I was really good to my mother. Whenever there was any wood to be chopped . . . I'd run right out and sharpen her axe.

She did everything she could to make me happy. One day after scrimping and saving she bought me a chalk-striped suit. It wasn't an expensive suit . . . In fact, the first rain washed away the chalk stripes . . . I should have known when I found that black-board eraser in the vest pocket.

I won't tell you how rough my childhood was, but my mother washed my clothes by beating them against a rock. While I was still in them.

———————

As a boy I spent most of my time trying to get my hands on a buck. It was up to all us Hopes to get in there and help out.

Things weren't much better for Dad in Cleveland than they'd been in England. Occasionally, he was called upon to go to New York to put a rose window in a church, but the skilled stone-cutting he knew how to do was going out of fashion. Jobs were hard to find.

Mom had her own ideas about meeting the family's obligations. She paid the butcher's bill when it came due, even if it meant walking through snow and sleet to do it. One of her darkest times was when she left her purse in a phone booth. It had eighty bucks in it. That eighty bucks was all the rent her roomers had paid her that week. She sent my brother Jack to look for it. While he was gone she prayed. Jack came back with the purse, but it was empty. Somebody had scooped it out and left it there. That was a rough blow. But no matter how rough things were, she clung to her standards, and they were higher than ours. All we cared about was getting our hooks on some dough to help her out.

———————

She used to say she'd never spoiled any of her children . . . and Dad would look at me and say, "All right then, who did?"

———————

Mom really enjoyed me . . . Whenever she was blue, she'd look at me and start laughing.

———————

ONE OF MY memories is her Saturday-night routine. She'd get out a big washtub and give us baths in the kitchen. She took us in order of our conduct for the week. If we'd been good, we got fresh water. That's why I was tan until I was thirteen. Nowadays, when I walk into a luxury hotel and see those gleaming bathroom fixtures, I remember that galvanized job in the kitchen, soap in my eyes, and Mother dunking us.

———————

I never had any money, but I always managed to give her a present on Mother's Day. It wasn't really a Mother's Day present; I'd just give her her Christmas present six months early.

Many's the time we didn't have a crumb of food in the house. We had to borrow a mouse from next door just to keep up a front.

We ate so seldom, whenever anybody in the family burped, instead of him saying, "Pardon me," we said, "Congratulations."

MY DAD'S NAME was William Henry Hope. In an effort to be funny, I've sometimes cracked, "When I was born, my mother said, 'William, get the doctor back. He's taken the baby and left the stork.'"

Dad was not only an artist with the stone-cutting tools, he was a happy man. He loved to live it up. He was popular, and a great entertainer. He was also well read. I remember professors from Case Western Reserve University in Cleveland would drop in to talk history with him.

My father was unemployed for ten years. But finally things took a turn for the better. He went out on strike.

The word "father" brings back a lot of memories to me . . . and there were times when I couldn't sit on those memories.

But I'm very grateful to my father . . . After all, when I was born, he and Mother took me into their house . . . and I was a total stranger at the time.

Once when my dad was teaching me a lesson out in the woodshed, the hairbrush slipped and hit me in the nose . . . The rest is history.

I have very fond memories of my father. When I got to the right age, he told me all about the birds and the bees . . . Of course, today he'd have to answer a few questions about Madonna.

AT ONE POINT, I sold papers on one of the corners of 102nd and Euclid. Three of my brothers had stands on the other corners. I had the Southwest

Grocery Store corner, Jack had the Cleveland Trust Company corner, Sid had the Marshall Drugstore corner, Fred the Standard Drugstore corner.

On my first day in school in Cleveland the other kids asked me, "What's your name?" When I said "Les Hope," they switched it to Hopeless. It got to be quite a rib and caused some scuffling and a few bloody ski-snoots for me.

I did so great in school; I'm still using the same device that got me all my top grades . . . idiot cards.

I used to love to tell jokes in school and I thought I was going over big till I found out all they were clapping were the erasers!

The tests were difficult for me because I couldn't copy off the other kids. Every time I looked over someone's shoulder my dunce cap fell off.

It took me so long to finish school, I got a B.A. . . . "Bachelor of Arthritis."

CHARLIE CHAPLIN IMITATIONS made me show-business-conscious. I'd put on my Chaplin makeup and walk duck-legged down to the corner past the firehouse. I twirled a rattan cane and wore flapping oversize, battered shoes. Amateur Charlie Chaplin contests had broken out in the country's theaters like a rash. I was so good at it that I was persuaded to enter a contest at Luna Park. To make sure I won, my brothers rounded up all the neighborhood kids and took them along to applaud. The man running the contest held his hand over the head of first one contestant, then another; then he cocked his ears for the volume of acclaim. When he held his hand over my head, the noise sounded like Indians screeching around a wagon train. The result was the No. 1 prize, a new cooking stove for Mom.

Our neighborhood was so tough, I never learned to walk . . . I started right out running.

If you didn't get in three fights a day you weren't trying. The closest thing I ever got to an award was getting my teeth back.

You've heard of the purple gang in Detroit. We were known as the black and blue gang. We fought a lot, but we didn't win much.

If you got to be sixteen and had half your ears and most of your teeth, you were a girl.

We had the typical gang. You know, Shorty, Fatso, Skinny, Stinky . . . Then there were the boys.

What tough kids we were . . . I remember how shocked we were when we found out Al Capone wasn't president.

We could smell a cop a mile away . . . and vice versa.

In those days, we had our old swimming hole until one day our parents decided it was too dirty to swim in. So we all got together and cleaned it up. Put in all new frogs.

Some people have a theory that poverty is a cause of juvenile delinquency. That's not true. My six brothers and I grew up in the poor section of Cleveland,

and we all turned out very well. I had a brother who was a meat packer . . . Another who was a metal manufacturer . . . Then there was a TV producer . . . a real estate man . . . a writer . . . a salesman . . . and I'm a comedian . . . Well, six out of seven ain't bad.

MY MOTHER TRIED TO be very broad-minded. She didn't approve of me hanging around the pool hall, but she was very tolerant about it. Every time I was leaving the house, she'd look at me and say, "Where is my little eight ball off to now?"

My pal Whitey Jennings and I were the whiz

kids of the Alhambra Pool Palace. My specialty was three-cushioned billiards. Whitey was a pool flash. Sometimes we even hustled the hustlers.

———————

I had another business when I was young. Our product was boomerangs. But we had to go out of business when they all came back.

Our boomerang was approved by Ralph Nader as the only product that recalls itself.

When I was a teenager, TV wasn't invented yet. My mother got the six o'clock news over the back fence.

I was well on my way to being a juvenile delinquent. When I was sixteen, I had more hubcaps than General Motors.

———————

WHITEY AND I were always prospecting around for ways to raise pocket money. The richest pay streak we hit was the picnic foot races. We were pretty good runners. Few kids our age could outrun us.
Sometimes there'd be a picnic at Luna Park and another at Euclid Beach the same day. We couldn't

be at both places at once, but we figured a way to lick the problem. If the grocers were having their picnic at Luna Park, we'd call the number of one of the picnic committee members and ask, "What time are you having your foot-racing events?"

The fellow might say, "Two-thirty. Why?"

"We're from the *Cleveland Press*," we'd say. "We wanted to take some photos. But two-thirty is too late. If you put them on at two o'clock, we'll send our cameraman out."

"Sure," he'd say. "Fine. Glad to have you."

Then we'd call the organization that was holding the competing picnic at Euclid Beach and arrange to have the races there postponed until three-thirty. When we'd arrive at Luna, the fellow in charge of the program would be waiting for the cameraman, but Whitey and I'd pressure him into starting the races without a photographer. "Let's get them over," we'd say. "We want to go swimming." So after a while he'd say, "O.K., we can't wait for that photographer all day."

Next we'd find out who was to start the races. Then we'd ask him, "How do you do your starting?"

"How does anybody start races?" he'd say. "On your marks, get set, go, of course."

When we'd caught his rhythm and were familiar with the interval between his "get set" and his "go" we'd start in that interval. That way we could count on a two-yard lead. With such a start, even Carl Lewis couldn't have caught us. Nobody noticed. They were smoking fat cigars and drinking beer. The first prize was fifteen dollars, the second ten. Whitey and I usually won first and second. Then we'd hurry out to Euclid Beach and knock off the same prizes there. No one ever believed more in the beneficial results of taking part in athletics than we did.

About that same time I took up boxing.

Some fighters have to be carried to their dressing rooms. I was the only fighter who had to be carried both ways.

I spent so much time on the canvas that they called me Rembrandt.

DESPITE ALL THE HARD times, and our attempts to make money, my mother was always there for us.

When I began to grow up and had theatrical ambitions, she took me to Keith's 105th Street in Cleveland to see Frank Fay. Frank was vaudeville's top monologist. He must have been pulling down $2,000 to $2,500 a week. That would be at least ten times as much today. He just stood there and talked to the audiences as if they were old friends.

After Frank had worked for a few minutes, Mother looked at me and said loudly, "He's not half as good as you."

"Sh-h-h," I said. "Please, Ma!"

The people near us looked at us as if we were goofy. Mom looked back at them defiantly and stared them down. Years later I had one of my biggest thrills when I came back to Cleveland and played that same theater. Mother was in the audience cheering. She knew.

————

My brother Fred and I were always trying to outdo each other. We'd be sibling rivals except neither of us knew what that meant.

One of my first jobs was in the butcher shop where my brother Fred worked. I was doing all right until one day he caught me putting meat in the hamburger . . . and that was it!

He was a great butcher, that's true. His thumbs weighed five pounds!

By the time I started in comedy, Fred had opened his own butcher shop. Fred was sure he'd make more money in the meat business than I'd make telling jokes. He was sure his baloney would outsell mine.

———

I WAS PAID ON Saturday nights. If I didn't think Fred had paid me enough, I'd wrap up some sweetbreads and take them over to my sweetheart, Mildred Rose-quist. She'd cook them and we'd have a feast. It was a chivalrous gesture, if I do say so myself. After all, how many fellows bring sweetbreads to their girls today?

Fred had a diabolical way of embarrassing me in front of my girl on Saturday nights. About seven-thirty Mildred would come over to the market to wait for me. I'd be trying to talk her into a session of watching the moonlight on the lake when Fred would ask in a conversational tone, "Les, would you mind taking the chicken guts downstairs?"

To say that this upset Mildred (and also my plans for a late date) is putting it mildly. Somehow, it didn't seem to fit in with romance, and it would have been a pleasure to boil, pluck, and disembowel Fred, too.

———————

It's funny how your outlook changes suddenly. One day anyone who plays with girls is a sissy, and the next day a sissy is anyone who doesn't.

I've always had a way with women . . . *their* way!

———————

BY THIS TIME I had become quite a dancer, even taught for a bit when I was about eighteen. Mildred and I had worked up a dance act and we played a few dates at such places as the Superior Theater. We'd make seven or eight bucks and I split it with her. "This is a little dance we learned in the living room," I'd tell the audience. Then we'd do that one, and I'd say, "This is a little dance we learned in the kitchen." Then we'd do that. We ended with, "This is a dance we learned in the parlor." The parlor dance was a buck dance. We saved it for last because it was our hardest and it left us exhausted.

That seven or eight bucks a performance was heady stuff. The applause went to my head even faster. I decided that the stage was my dish. Once I decided that, I was a pushover for it. I'd gone to Fairmount Grammar School, to Fairmount Junior High, then to East High. After a year and a half at East High I quit.

I didn't waste too much time thinking about going to college. I plunged right into a career . . . unemployment.

My mother wanted me to go to Ohio State. My father just wanted me to go.

I'm proud of my state. Ohio has a lot of schools. I know. I avoided most of them.

I PLANNED TO TAKE Mildred with me when I went on the road, but Mildred's mother was small-minded about it. (Another way of putting it is to say that Mildred's mother got the notion that I wasn't the divinity-student type and she refused to trust her daughter on theatrical tours with me.) So before long, I gave Mildred up.

Mildred's mother said that even if we got out-of-town bookings—which she seriously doubted—her daughter couldn't go on tour with me unchaperoned. I should never have let her see the act, but she did, and she hid Mildred until she was sure I was out of town. Having lost one partner, I picked up another, Lloyd Durbin, a dancer I had known around 105th and Euclid.

We traveled by bus. The audiences were tough. So were the living conditions. We were paid off in lean bellies and laughs.

———————

I played in one tough town . . . on the marquee they had my name, age, and beneficiary.

I stuck my head out of the curtain to look at the audience . . . The audience stuck its head out from behind a seat and looked at me.

We all cooked in our dressing rooms. During her number the prima donna sniffed the air and screamed, "Oh my gosh . . . my ham."

The manager was swell; he gave us fifteen minutes during intermission . . . to get out of town.

It was one of those newfangled shows . . . You know, without scenery, without dialogue, without plot . . . without audience.

There are long lines at the box office every night . . . people asking for their money back.

———————

I WAS MAKING FORTY dollars a week and sending twenty home to my mother to help out. I don't know how I lived on twenty dollars a week, but I did it. For one thing, the dollar went a long way in those days. It goes a long way now too—all the way to Washington, D.C.—but in those days you were allowed to feel it, see it, even use it.

———————

I've always worked for a living. At eight, I had a paper route . . . At twelve, I worked in my brother's butcher shop . . . At eighteen, I was out on the road singing and dancing . . . and at nineteen, I was back on my paper route.

As we had so many times before, back we went to Mom's lemon meringue pie and stories of my brothers while we waited for our agent to find us something. Finally, he wired back that he could get us three days at New Castle, Pennsylvania, at fifty dollars. We were the third act on the bill. It only had three.

About this same time, I decided I'd do something different and relaxing. Golf was recommended, but the first time I tried golf I was a total failure. I went out for a few rounds in 1927, when I was twenty-four, at Highland Park, a public course in Cleveland. I couldn't advance the ball. Some shots I'd whiff, some I'd just scuff along the ground. Foursomes of women were playing through me. I just didn't seem to have any feel for the game, so I said the hell with it and quit.

Golf is a lesson in humility.

Golf is misery with a caddy.

Bowling has one advantage over golf. You rarely lose a ball.

BY THIS TIME, I had decided to take a chance on my own. I started doing my single in Cleveland, and the best I could do was a few dollars a night, and that was when I could get work. Bookings were scarce and I was getting desperate. I tried anything. I changed my name from Lester to Bob; it sounded a little chummier, but I still starved for a while. I was told Chicago was the place for me. Maybe it was the agent's way of getting rid of me. So I moved on to Chicago, but Chicago in 1928 wasn't ready for me. I couldn't get in anybody's door.

———————

Jobs didn't come easy. For months at a time, I forgot what kind of work I was out of.

By the time I did say something funny, half the audience would laugh and wake up the other half.

———————

I WAS STANDING in front of the Woods Theater Building listening to my empty stomach growling and wondering whether to give up and hop a bus for Cleveland when Charlie Cooly walked up. I'd gone to school with Charlie. He asked how I was doing. When I told him, he took me to see another Charlie, Charlie Hogan, who booked a lot of theaters around Chicago. "How'd you like to play the West Englewood Theater Decoration Day?" Hogan asked me. "Would twenty-five dollars be all right?"

I just managed to say, "I'll take it," without bursting into tears. The West Englewood had three shows daily. I emceed them and did my act.

After the second show, the manager said, "You're to open at the Stratford, Sunday.

"Charlie Hogan called me," he said. "He asked me how you were doing. I told him you were O.K., so he told me to tell you he's putting you in as master of ceremonies at the Stratford for three weeks."

———————————

I used to struggle to make ends meet. I wouldn't have had anything to eat if it wasn't for the stuff the audience threw at me.

I worked in vaudeville all summer . . . I made seven thousand dollars . . . in vegetables alone. Vaudeville . . . that's French for ham and eggs with scenery. It was the first time a backdrop ever stole the show. I remember when I used to sneak into the theater . . . now I just sneak out.

All the while I was on the stage an usher ran up and down the aisles yelling, "Get your program . . . get your program . . . you don't know who to blame without a program."

I was paying the spotlight man five bucks to keep me out of it.

Two kids were caught sneaking in . . . we fixed them . . . we made them see the whole show.

The show closed to recast the audience.

———————

THOSE THREE WEEKS at the Stratford turned into six months, so I began to run out of material. Trying to get laughs with nothing to get them with was valuable. However, when I left the Stratford it was easy to put an act together using material gathered from my stay there.

As a partner, I'd signed up Louise Troxell, a girl I'd met around Chicago and had developed into a foil. She was quick and intelligent, but I'd trained her to hide that. All she had to do was to walk on and stand there looking beautiful while I told a story, then feed me lines. She'd come out holding a little bag in her hand and say:

"How do you do?" I'd say, "What do you have in your little bag?" and she'd say, "Mustard." And I'd say, "What's the idea?" And she'd say, "You can never tell when you're going to meet a ham."

As anyone can see, this started the routine off in sophisticated fashion.

———————

I'll never forget those one-night stands, going from town to town. Always on the go. . . and they never caught me either.

With my act, I qualified for combat pay during peace time.

We didn't know what vegetable we'd have for dinner until after the show.

I'm gonna have six people in the act with me . . . two to watch me . . . and four to keep an eye on the audience.

I time my jokes . . . in fact, this is the tenth time for most of them.

Everybody who saw my act told me I'd go far . . .
The manager of the theater told me I'd go far . . .
Not only that . . . he stood out in the road and
pointed.

———————

THEN WE OPENED at the Inter-State Time in Fort
Worth, Texas. I did the same act I'd done in
Chicago. I worked fast, snappy, and impish. It was
my idea to tell the audience, "You've got to get my
stuff fast because that's the way I sell it." I'd been a
showstopper with this tempo. But in Fort Worth I
laid a Texas-size egg. Theater owner Bob O'Donnell
gave me some good advice: "Slow down, fancy pants,
people here take things a little slower." I learned a lot
about how to work an audience.

———————

The people sure are demanding a lot of
entertainment at one time now . . . The last time I
played vaudeville . . . I had to do my act while the
picture was on.

I'll never forget the last time I played there . . . I
hope the audience does.

I remember one review I got in a Philadelphia paper. The critic wrote, "Bob Hope will go places. That's fine with me as long as Philadelphia isn't one of the places."

There were thousands waiting at the stage door, cheering madly, daring me to come out.

I really love the stage . . . Why, if I had to work for nothing, I'd quit tomorrow.

IN 1930 I WAS on the vaudeville circuit with the Diamond Brothers, a comedy act. During the summer we played the northern route—Winnipeg, Calgary, Minneapolis, Seattle, and Tacoma. We did matinees and evening shows, so there was nothing for me to do during the morning except sit around the hotel lobbies. I used to see the Diamonds come clattering through the lobby every day with their golf bags. One day, in Seattle, they invited me to come along. I borrowed a set of clubs and started hitting the ball pretty well. I got hooked on golf that day. I've been addicted to it ever since.

I hit so many divots that two ants nearby said, "Let's get on the ball or he'll kill us."

I play golf every chance I get. The world needs more laughter.

I play golf in the eighties. Any hotter I won't play.

Take nine strokes off your score. Skip the last hole.

If golf is relaxing . . . you're not playing it right.

IN 1932, I appeared on Broadway in *Ballyhoo*. But my first major recognition, from critics and the public, came in 1933 for my wisecracking role as Huckleberry Haines in the highly successful Broadway musical *Roberta*. *Roberta* ran from November 1933 through July 14, 1934. It gave me the chance to watch a genius, Jerome Kern, close up. I'd have worked that show for nothing (almost) to stand in the wings and listen to his music.

The girls in *Roberta* were beautiful and I was young and on the lookout. I also had a Scottie dog who was a surefire girl magnet. Once I got a load of them, I went out and bought a bottle of an after-shave lotion that was supposed to make a man smell like old leather.

About this time I remember being in Atlantic City helping Jack Benny celebrate a new radio contract he'd just landed. Canada Dry had promised to give him six thousand, six hundred dollars a show, so we all had a drink on him. To me, that's a standout because I used to think: Wouldn't it be amazing to make a thousand dollars a week? If I ever made a thousand a week I don't think I'd talk to anybody. How could you make a thousand dollars a week? If I'd told them back home that I was making four hundred a week they'd think I'd been robbing a bank and was hiding out.

———

MY PERSONAL LIFE changed during my run in *Roberta*. One of my co-stars, George Murphy, took me to see a sultry young singer, Dolores Reade, who was appearing at the Vogue Club. It was love at first song. I was hooked. She was the most beautiful gal I'd ever seen. After a brief courtship, we married in February 1934.

Once *Roberta* closed, Dolores left the supper-club circuit and agreed to be part of my vaudeville act. Next, I opened in the Broadway musical *Say When* (1934), followed by the 1936 edition of *The Ziegfeld Follies*, in which I shared the spotlight with Fanny Brice. My success in *Follies* led me to a role in *Red, Hot, and Blue* (1936) with Ethel Merman and Jimmy Durante.

Although I had made several short comedies for Warner Brothers in New York, and done some radio, it was my performance in *Red, Hot, and Blue* that opened the door to my first major feature film for Paramount Pictures, *The Big Broadcast of 1938*. That film got me some attention in Hollywood and a theme song, "Thanks for the Memory," which I used for the rest of my career.

After I traveled to Hollywood to film *The Big Broadcast of 1938*, I continued doing my radio show—*The Woodbury Soap Show*—via transcontinental hook-up. When I closed out that radio season with Woodbury, I signed with Lucky Strike for a revue originating in Hollywood. I had a ten-minute monologue.

———————

Out here in Hollywood you can go to a restaurant, theater, or oil station and make believe you're in any country you like.

A tour of Hollywood is like a trip around the world . . . It might cost a little more than the real thing, but think of the time I save.

The big craze in phony atmosphere now the rage in Hollywood is the Hawaiian mania. I sat in one place with my girl and felt like a castaway in an *Esquire* cartoon . . . only there was plenty of food, and my thoughts were cleaner.

This place was just crammed full of tropical atmosphere. The headwaiter came up and asked me if I would like to sit under a palm tree, by a waterfall, near the parrots, by a babbling brook, balmy breeze, cloudburst, thunderstorm, hurricane, or volcano! I said, "Give me a table by the weatherman, so I will know what is going to happen next."

———————

M Y NEXT PICTURE was *College Swing*, then *The Cat and the Canary*, and then my first *Road* picture, *The Road to Singapore* with Bing Crosby and Dorothy Lamour. Paramount had been planning the movie for George Burns and Gracie Allen. Because Burns and Allen were not available, they tapped Fred MacMurray and Jack Oakie, who were also booked. So it ended up starring me, Bing, and Dorothy. Nobody thought this would lead to a series, but it was hugely successful at the box office, and the studio wanted more. Most of the *Road* pictures have the same plot: Crosby chasing Lamour, me chasing Crosby, and the public behind us—gaining all the time.

In 1939, I was asked to host the Oscars.

I don't want them to give me the Academy Award. I would be happy if Paramount would just give me a dressing room.

I received an award from all the theater managers. It wasn't exactly an award. It was more of an ultimatum.

All the directors are award-conscious. One of them told me that if I ever became conscious I might win the award.

Next year I'm a sure bet for the Academy Awards. Well, anyway . . . place or show.

I just finished a picture that would positively win the award, but it hasn't been released yet . . . and by next year at this time the award committee will have forgotten all about it.

Ferdinand the Bull would have won the Academy Award, but he claimed that Disney gave him a bum steer.

Mickey Mouse was in line to win the award, but as usual he wound up in a hole.

I would have won the Academy Award if not for one thing . . . my pictures.

SOON AFTER THE AWARDS, WWII broke out. In May 1941, I went to March Field, California—along with a group of other performers—to do a radio show for airmen stationed there. What an audience it was. The show was produced in our established radio format with an opening monologue, cast-member comedy, music, a guest star sketch, and the usual commercials. The only thing that was new was adapting our comedy to a military context.

It was a great success. We made a point of researching the military lingo, favorite watering holes, and commanding officers' names. The stern military regime evoked laughs, as did the soldiers' resentments, hardships, and habits. They laughed at me, but most of all they laughed at themselves. This was the beginning of my love for the GI. I decided to take the cast of my radio show to the San Diego Naval Station next (sailors like to laugh, too).

———————

Yes sir, here we are broadcasting at the naval base at San Diego. Everyone down here is in the Navy. In fact, a man who doesn't roll when he walks has to register as an alien.

I was really thrilled when I arrived in San Diego. The mayor met me on the City Hall steps and gave me the key to the washroom. Then an officer stepped up to me and said he had orders to congratulate me in advance on behalf of the people of Tijuana. I said, "But I'm not going to Mexico," and he said, "I know . . . and we appreciate what you're doing to help the good neighbor policy."

My girl is so crazy about sailors; she thinks Marine is something for the eyes.

But things are really booming here in San Diego. San Diego . . . that's Spanish for try and find a place to live. The city is really crowded. In fact, it's now within five thousand of being as big as they used to claim it was.

But they've been very nice to us here today. An ensign showed us around . . . an ensign . . . That's a second lieutenant that can swim.

THE YEAR 1942 was a year of sacrifice in the United States. On the home front, not a man, woman, or child was exempt from the war effort. Women flocked to the factories to take over jobs left vacant by men going to war; many of these jobs

became assembly lines that made America's war machinery.

You know, it certainly is confusing the way women are taking men's places in jobs these days. A fellow doesn't know whether to just say "So long" to the night watchman or try to kiss him goodnight.

One woman cabdriver brought her baby along and sat him on her lap . . . It's really great . . . That's the first time I ever saw a steering wheel used for driving and a teething ring at the same time.

But women are doing their bit, too. The women say they can do any job a man can. Last week, a woman welder threw both knees out of joint trying to hold herself on her own lap.

Women have made a new life for themselves . . . And be it ever so humble, there's no place like Lockheed.

You can tell the women are working on the P-38's . . . I saw one yesterday and both its tails were clipped.

Of course, with their wives working in airplane factories, the husbands have to eat dinner out . . . unless they wanna pay 'em time and a half for overtime.

Americans were asked to make do with less. Wartime rationing was a consequence of this war. The military had first priority on supplies. Signs of the times were ration books, red meat tokens, and A, B, C, and T gasoline stickers on the windshields of cars. Things taken for granted were now unavailable—sugar, coffee, chewing gum, cigarettes. There were very few complaints. Sacrifice was part of everyone's patriotic contribution.

I had a little trouble getting here because of the gas rationing. You've heard of those A cards, and B cards, and X cards? Well, they gave me one marked "Please use an eye dropper!"

One thing I like about Chicago . . . there are no shortages here. You can get all the sugar you want. I went into a restaurant and said, "I'll have three

lumps in my coffee!" . . . And you know what I got?
Four lumps in the alley.

On Broadway, a panhandler walked up to me and
said, "Hey, buddy . . . got five dollars for a cuppa
coffee?" I said, "Whaddya need five dollars for . . .
Coffee only costs a nickel!" He said, "I know, but
you have to tip pretty heavy these days to get an
extra lump of sugar!!!"

Everything is so scarce. I wanted to buy some
pepper, so the grocer got a pair of tweezers and
asked, "How many?"

You should see the way they slice the baloney these
days. I wouldn't say they slice it thin, but when you
get through wrapping it, you can't tell which is the
cellophane.

It used to be that you had to have a diamond ring to
propose to a girl. Now all you have to do is snap a
rubber band in her face.

It used to be a guy would slug you with a piece of
rubber hose and take away your wad . . . Now

they slug you with a wad and take away your rubber hose.

Remember those automobile rides when the girl used to walk home to save her reputation? Now they both walk home to save their tires!

———————

HOLLYWOOD WENT TO WAR in a big way. Some of its biggest stars enlisted. Those who were not in the armed forces were giving their time, talent, and resources on the home front. If they were not busy with bond rallies, they were serving up coffee and conversation at canteens in New York and Hollywood.

The Hollywood Canteen was on a side street off Hollywood Boulevard. Movies stars—such as Bette Davis, Lana Turner, Hedy Lamarr, Dorothy Lamour, and Betty Grable—pitched in, entertained, waited on tables, washed dishes, and danced with the soldiers and sailors passing through. Dinah Shore and I washed dishes with Vice President Henry Wallace, who wanted to show what a clean politician he was.

———————

I arrived here from the Hollywood Canteen . . . and that canteen is a wonderful place. The Brown Derby sends over food, Chapman's sends over ice cream, the Mayflower sends over doughnuts . . . (Pause) . . . When I left, two Marines were waiting around to see what Earl Carroll would send over.

I know one soldier who got the greatest thrill of his life at the Hollywood Canteen. He got a kiss from Hedy Lamarr . . . and it didn't really bother him for long. All I know is that when he came to, he was already AWOL for two days.

There was one big fat hostess there. Boy, was she fat! One soldier waltzed with her for fifteen minutes before he found out there was a sailor on the other side doing the rhumba.

I helped out in the kitchen . . . Hedy Lamarr, Dorothy Lamour, and Paulette Goddard were there, too . . . I was supposed to do the dishwashing, but with them around I was cooking.

The stars wait on the tables and act as busboys. There was such a big crowd of servicemen there last night, Nelson Eddy spent two hours in the kitchen, trying to stretch his shortenin' bread.

I must explain to all civilian listeners that the Hollywood Canteen is a place strictly for enlisted men, and no officers are allowed in. In fact, it's like a crap game after taps have blown.

You should see the crowds waiting to get into the canteen . . . One guy waited in line so long, he finally said to the fella in front of him, "I don't think I'll ever get in." The other guy said, "What are you complaining about? . . . I'm Sergeant York."

One soldier went to the Hollywood Canteen and danced with Hedy Lamarr, Betty Grable, and Lana Turner . . . I don't know if it affected him or not, but he was a little late getting back to camp . . . It was Tuesday before an antiaircraft unit in San Diego could shoot him down.

Everything's changed in Hollywood, though. All lights are dimmed out . . . Everybody's driving under thirty-five, and the wolves from Hollywood and Vine are now out at gate number five at Lock-heed.

And this Hollywood Canteen is awfully popular . . . Soldiers come in here every night. After looking at top sergeants all day, you can't blame them for staring at the glamour girls here . . . They're a sight for sore GIs.

But it's swell for the fellows . . . There's really a lot of USO girls in Hollywood . . . USO . . . Use Slacks Only.

ONE OF THE MOVIE industry's most successful war efforts was the Hollywood Victory Caravan, a special train carrying some of the nation's most popular entertainers all doing what they could to help the war effort. We crossed the country, rehearsing on the way, for the Washington kickoff of a two-week whistle-stop tour for the Army and Navy relief funds.

The show was a three-hour variety package of popular songs, dances, comedy sketches, dramatic scenes and readings, even operatic arias. All the stars, including our little group—me, Frances Langford, and Jerry Colonna—were invited to a White House lawn party given by Eleanor Roosevelt.

We all came in on a special train called the Victory Train. I don't know why they call it the Victory Train . . . I sat next to Merle Oberon for three thousand miles and I'm still calling her Miss Oberon.

I just arrived on that Victory Train with all the Hollywood stars . . . What movie stars on that train . . . Cary Grant, Joan Bennett, Claudette Colbert, Joan Blondell, Charlie Boyer, James Cagney . . . It was really a tough trip . . . You were lucky if you could mention your own pictures once every half hour.

We're living right on the train during the whole trip . . . A few of the stars are so tight that they're even doing their own laundry . . . But most of them are willing to pay my price . . . But they made me quit . . . Somebody complained I was clogging up the drinking fountain.

Boy, what beautiful girls on that train . . . I walked up to Irene Dunne and said, "Honey, remember me, Bob Hope?" . . . She looked at me and said, "I don't remember the name . . . but the drool is familiar."

You should have seen those beautiful stars . . . I couldn't help staring at them . . . In fact, my eyes popped out so far the bag under one eye turned to the other and said, "We'd better get packed, it looks like they're leaving for the weekend."

The engineer let me steer for a while, and he told me to keep my eyes on the road . . . A few minutes later, Joan Blondell, Merle Oberon, and Joan Bennett walked by . . . I won't say I took my eyes off the road . . . But that's the first time a Santa Fe train ever climbed Pike's Peak, crossed the Great Lakes without a bridge, and picked up three passengers in Alaska.

I had a wonderful seat right next to Barbara Stanwyck . . . But around Kansas City . . . Robert Taylor began getting heavy.

There was one beautiful glamour girl on the train . . . I didn't remember her name . . . But her sweater was familiar.

I tried to kiss a girl going around a sharp bend . . . When I got my head in out of the window . . . three cows were waving at me fondly.

All the other male actors were jealous of me because throughout the trip I had all the exciting girls to myself . . . But soon I tired of it . . . After all, how long can a guy read *Esquire.*

We practically have to live on the train because we're traveling continuously . . . and Groucho Marx has come to look on it as his home from now on . . . I found that out when I tried to climb into my berth last night . . . What a place for a victory garden!

Then we stopped in Washington and it's really a lovely place . . . Yes sir . . . Eleanor ought to see that town.

Glad to be in Washington, D.C. . . . D.C. . . . That's French for Damned Crowded.

Washington is really crowded . . . You have to get a priority number to play a pinball machine.

Washington is the toughest place in the world to find a place to live . . . Ask any Republican.

WE WERE ON a roll. Following the Victory Caravan, Frances Langford, Jerry Colonna, Tony Romano, Patty Thomas, and I were off to entertain more GIs—sixty-five shows at a variety of military bases and hospitals. September found us Alaska-bound. From there, we headed for Galena and then to Nome. When the crowd of GIs gathered to hear our act, the applause was muffled by heavy gloves, but the laughs echoed off the frost of their breath.

This is our first trip up north and the Army has really taken care of us. They gave us a plane that was flown by a four-star general . . . Pershing . . . I knew it was an old plane when I saw the pilot sitting behind me wearing goggles and a scarf.

This is Bob "Alaskan Army Base" Hope telling you to always use Pepsodent and you'll never leave your teeth lying in a chair and get bit-ka when you sit-ka.

I tell you, it's really great up here in Alaska—and they were certainly glad to see me. The minute I stepped out of the plane they started following me across the field applauding and applauding . . . Gee, who'd have thought *seals* listened to this show . . . or maybe it was my *herringbone* slacks.

Then we all got in an Army truck and rode up to the Post. I got out of the truck first and started to make a speech to a bunch of the soldiers. Then Frances Langford got out of the truck right behind me. The doctor says in a few months you won't be able to notice these footprints on my face!

But there was one old sergeant who's been stationed up here in Alaska for three straight enlistments. When Frances got out of the truck, he just looked at her and said, "What is it?"

Then he looked at me . . . and that didn't help any.

An igloo . . . that's like an Auto Court—only "quick frozen."

Ours was half a ton of ice cubes all piled up with a hole in the top. For a door, there was a pistachio Good Humor.

It is so cold up here I couldn't ever tell what time it was. Every time I'd pull out my watch, it'd just start rubbing its hands together and hollering, "Either I get mittens or I quit!"

It was so chilly that when I started to go to bed that night, I had to use an ice pick to untie my tie.

———

WHEN I RETURNED HOME, I was asked again to host the March 1943 Academy Award ceremonies. The movies during this time made a conscious effort to acknowledge the heroism and sacrifice of people everywhere. The film business was serving well on the war front and the home front.

———

This is my fourth visit presenting awards . . . When it comes to an Oscar, I can dish it out but I just can't take it!

You know what an Oscar is? . . . That's just something that got a deferment from the scrap metal drive!

Glad to be here at the Actor's USO . . . USO . . . "Undying Struggle for Oscars!"

The draft really has hit the movie studios. In fact, when they give a new leading man a screen test, they don't bother with any long love scenes . . . They just photograph him to show he can stand in a vertical position and the camera moves in for a close-up of the 4-F on his draft card!

Gary Cooper and Greer Garson have been getting all the swell dramatic roles this year. How can I win an Oscar making those *Road* pictures over at Paramount? . . . I'm not an actor . . . I'm a traveling salesman.

DeMille had a little accident . . . You know how he sits down whenever he wants? Well, yesterday the guy that carries around his chair was drafted!

It's awfully nice of these people to come here every year and keep Bette Davis company. Of course, a great many male stars are in the Army now . . . In fact, most of the leading men are now out leading men!

Ladies and gentlemen, at this point I am honored, greatly honored, to introduce one of the best-loved figures in the entertainment field for the past quarter of a century. A man who served in the last war, and who is serving in the present war by being the guiding light of that outstanding show, *This Is the Army*—Mr. Irving Berlin! Before turning the microphone over to Irving, I'd like to say that right now, Berlin is in our Army . . . Let's hope that it won't be long before our Army is in Berlin!

IN 1943, I set out with our small USO troupe (Frances Langford, Tony Romano, and Jack Pepper—Colonna was unavailable) to visit U.S. military facilities in Europe and North Africa. What we caught from the guys' laughter was the spirit of the mission. It was contagious—there seemed to be no limit to our energies.

I've just arrived from the States. You know, that's where Churchill lives. Well, he doesn't exactly live there . . . he just goes back to deliver Mrs. Roosevelt's laundry.

Hi ya, fellow tourists. Well, I'm very happy to be here, but of course, I'm leaving as soon as I finish the show. But this is a great country, Africa . . . this is Texas with Arabs.

Our troops in North Africa are something. What hardships they went through! Night after night they went without sleep . . . always alert . . . always keeping their eye on the objective . . . finally Frances Langford pulled her shade down.

What country that North Africa is. I won't say it's dusty there . . . but it's the only place I know where you spit cement.

THE USO TRIP had quite an effect on me. I realized that any contribution I was making was minimal. I was offering time and laughs—the men and women fighting the war were offering up their lives. They taught me what sacrifice was all about.

On March 11, I had the opportunity to emcee the Gridiron Dinner honoring President Roosevelt in Washington, D.C. I was nervous.

Good evening, Mr. President, distinguished guests, I was late getting here because we flew through mud all the way, and then coming in from the airport I was on the bottom layer of the taxi. But I'm delighted to be here. I've always wanted to be invited to one of these dinners, and my invitation has been a long time in coming. I thought I had been vetoed by [Alben] Barkley [a senator who was giving the president a hard time in Congress]. Perhaps I shouldn't mention Alben here . . . it's too much like talking about Frank Sinatra to Bing Crosby.

I think I should apologize to our president for some of the things I've said on radio. Especially about Mrs. Roosevelt. Like when Churchill and Roosevelt were discussing [war] campaign strategy, they talked about the enemy and how to keep Eleanor out of the crossfire.

Tuesday, June 6, 1944, was D-Day. I did a special tribute to the men landing on Normandy Beach. Thanks to their sacrifice, the tide in Europe was turning, but there was still a major part of the war to be fought—in the Pacific. I couldn't wait to finish the movie that I was working on at the time, *Princess and the Pirate,* so I could visit our troops fighting in the South Pacific. Our first stop was Hawaii, then on to countless islands in the Pacific.

What an island. When the tide comes in, you guys should get submarine pay. You're not defending this place, are you? Let them take it, it'll serve them right.

I'll admit that I was a little scared when we started the trip. To tell the truth, I held up the first takeoff half a day before I even got into the plane. Every time they started the motors, my hands pulled my rip cord.

We did a lot of flying over the Pacific, and once we had to make a forced landing. A forced landing . . .

that's an aviation term meaning, "Why didn't I go to church last Sunday?"

You should see those jungles. They're impenetrable. I said to the pilot, "Gosh, they must use a lot of bulldozers to cut a path through that thick underbrush." He said, "Bulldozers, nothing. They just put a chowhound at one end of the jungle . . . build a mess hall on the other, and the suction takes it from there."

Some of those islands we landed on were really little. One island we hit was so small, the gophers hadda take turns coming up.

The weather down there is like it is here. Of course, they have a slight sprinkle now and then. Light sprinkle. That's South Pacific for "Man the boats, boys . . . the island disappeared again."

But when we got back at the end of the trip, I was really a veteran. I said to the pilot, "Well, here we are safe and sound after thirty-five thousand miles." And he said, "Yes, Mr. Hope . . . you can open your eyes and take a breath now."

What a beautiful swamp you have here. This'd be a good spot to build a cesspool . . . you wanna hide something from your draft board, this is the place to do it.

_____

Shortly after my return, the presidential campaign was in full swing. Franklin D. Roosevelt was running for an unprecedented fourth term with Harry S. Truman as his running mate. Their opponent was New York governor Thomas E. Dewey. FDR won by a landslide.

But then came the broadcast of April 12. The whole nation mourned the death of one of the world's greatest leaders, Franklin D. Roosevelt. And if we were nervous about Harry S. Truman, a Missouri haberdasher, taking over the reins of the country, he soon won our confidence.

_____

Truman could shake your hand and measure you for a suit at the same time.

It's true, he was a haberdasher by trade. If it weren't for him, the suit on the Lincoln Memorial never would have fit.

He made great suits. But if he knew you were a Republican, it wasn't wise to let him measure your inseam.

Truman tried to be nice about his daughter's singing. I was there the day Margaret found out her father didn't wear earmuffs because of the cold.

He once wrote a nasty letter to a music critic who had given his daughter a bad review. It helps to have a father who's tone deaf.

Harry didn't care about image. That's because he had a weapon that could bring the world to its knees—Margaret Truman's singing.

Truman rules the country with an iron fist . . . the same way he plays the piano.

―――――――――

EVERYTHING WAS HAPPENING at once in the war. The Italians captured Mussolini and hung his mistress upside down beside him. The Russians captured the Reichstag in Berlin and Hitler turned a gun on himself. We were entertaining the servicemen and

women at the U.S. Naval Training Center in Ocean-
side, California, when we got the news about the victory in Europe.

The U.S. soldiers in Europe didn't know if they
were going to be shipped back to the States or the
meat grinder in the Pacific. The government
decided they should have a little entertainment in
the meantime. We did our first show at Albert Hall
in London on the Fourth of July in front of ten thousand GIs.

This is Bob (don't ask me where I am because I
don't know, and even if I did know, I couldn't tell,
because it's a military secret) Hope saying that if
you soldiers use a certain dentifrice (that's BBC for
toothpaste) it will preserve those pearly whites
under your snouts, so that you can eat those good
old brussels sprouts.

Well, it's certainly great to be here in jolly olde . . .
that's England. England is the place that Churchill
visits when he leaves America. That man travels so
much. He's been in Casablanca more than
Humphrey Bogart. He goes to America especially

to see Mr. Roosevelt . . . he can see Mrs. Roosevelt anywhere.

We flew over to England by the same route Churchill took. It was easy. All we had to do was follow the cigar ashes.

It was a great trip over; we had a few drinks in Canada and flew blind all the way. It got so foggy on the way, the seagulls were walking.

When we got to Scotland, it was so foggy people were using instruments to get into bed—but we finally landed in England, the one free spot in Europe. There's occupied France, occupied Poland . . . only the taxicabs are occupied in England.

I guess this is the first time I ever laid a powdered egg. But I don't mind powdered eggs . . . they're great stuff after shaving. Can you imagine, the people in America don't have them. They've got to put up with those old-fashioned types of eggs, you know, the ones with the shells that crack.

And the way they drive here! Everybody drives on the wrong side of the street . . . just like California.

I love those chemist's shops, you know, the drug-stores, fine drugstores—you can even buy a tire inside, or a vacuum cleaner, or even a malted milk.

I love the women here. Every one is in the services or the factories. You can't take them out for a time, they want time and a half. And I've never seen so many women in uniform . . . you've got to get up awfully close to them before you know whether to whistle or salute.

The girls I like are the Wrens, you know, the English Waves . . . down to the sea in slips. Then there are a lot of American WAACs here. I had a date with one the other day. She must have come from the WAACs museum. I met her during a night alert. Boys, you haven't lived until you've had a WAAC out in the blackout with the flak out. If you get a chance, better back out. You can't kid about the women's service, though. They're very strict. The worst form of punishment is to send a girl to the guardhouse with ten new hats and no mirror. I took one to a pub one night. You know what a pub is . . . that's an ashtray with chairs. We had a little beer.

The beer here is weaker than a utility girdle. I ought to know, mine split in three places . . . of course, I should have never gone to those places.

How do you do, fellow tourists. This is Bob Hope, telling you guys that I rushed here as fast as I could because I heard they were going to ration fraternization. I stopped off in Paris on my way here; they had quite a few artists there, sketching the girls in a show I saw. I thought I'd try it, but they threw me out—they said no fair tracing.

Last night I slept in the barracks. You know what the barracks are—a crap game with a roof. What a place to meet professional gamblers. I won't say they were loaded, but it's the first time I ever saw dice leave skid marks. A discharge—that's a little piece of paper that changes a lieutenant's name from "sir" to "stinky." Soldiers are real strong. I walked in with a blonde on one arm and a brunette on the other. Two minutes later, no blonde, no brunette, no arms.

———

PEOPLE OFTEN ASK ME, "Why did you go on so many of those trips?" The answer is this:

Wherever I go, boys say to me, "Hi, Bob! Saw you in Africa," or "Saw you in the South Pacific," or "Saw you in Alaska. And it meant so much to us."

This is also the reason why so many other entertainers did the same thing. Ask Jack Benny, Danny Kaye, Betty Hutton, or hundreds of other USO troupers. They'll also tell you that you can work an audience and pull down twenty thousand bucks, but if the audience doesn't like you, you won't be happy with all that money. But if you work an audience for nothing and you're a hit and you feel that electricity crackle back and forth between you, you're happy. Being there is definitely a kick.

In 1945, the war was finally over.

———————

This is Bob "Broadcasting for future civilians at the Santa Ana Separation Center, California" Hope, telling all you guys who'll soon be eating home cooking to use Pepsodent, and when Mom hands you a chicken leg, you'll be able to dent 'er . . . if your teeth don't have a separation in the center.

I knew the troops would be glad to see me. I said, "Look at me, fellas. These are the kind of clothes you'll be wearing when you get home!" Fifty guys re-enlisted.

Right now these fellas are interested in good jobs . . . I know they are . . . I saw a couple of guys following one down the street in Santa Ana.

One Air Force colonel went out and bought a farm. He had been in action so long, every morning before the chickens started laying eggs, he called 'em into the chicken coop and briefed 'em.

And it wasn't only the military that faced a lot of changes. All the war workers are heading back home . . . They're leaving just like they came, with their mattresses piled on top of their cars . . . There's one small difference . . . Going back, the mattresses are stuffed with dollar bills.

And some of these workers had really been on the job a long time . . . We met one fellow who'd worked on the P-38 so long, instead of ears, he had two tails sticking out back from his head.

I don't know how much money those war workers made, but I saw a jalopy going down the highway and it was towing a branch office of the Bank of America.

And you can get all the gas you want now . . . I filled my car up . . . started my motor . . . and one cylinder turned to the other and said, "Isn't this wonderful, Herman? . . . We can go wading again."

And the new gas is really powerful. You can tell the difference right away. With the postwar gas, when you hit a pedestrian *he falls down*.

Yes sir, all the gas you want is really great . . . In fact, they're not saying "Fill 'er up" anymore . . . They say, "Splash it over . . . I wanna wade in it."

Here I am starting my eighth year for the same sponsor . . . I reenlisted . . . If I finish this season, I'll have more hash marks than Nimitz.

I'm really thrilled tonight, because they requested me to keep appearing before military audiences . . . What I didn't like about it . . . The request came from civilian audiences.

When we flew over New York, I felt a real tug at my heart . . . My girdle had caught in the airplane door.

I was really glad to get back to Hollywood . . . I kissed my wife, I kissed my kids, then rushed out and kissed the street cleaner . . . He said, "That's not necessary anymore . . . The cigarette shortage is over!"

But it really is wonderful now that the country's at peace . . . I know the war is really over . . . Yesterday I saw a butcher smiling.

Things sure have changed since the war is over . . . Now when you ask for a chocolate bar and the man says, "Nuts?" . . . he doesn't mean you.

And thank goodness, the cigarette shortage is over . . . I've got housemaid's knee from racing with the vacuum cleaner to see who'll inhale first.

And it's wonderful to be able to go into a restaurant now and hear the waitress say, "What'll you have?" instead of "Take it or leave it."

They say we can get some of those things we've always wanted now . . . But don't you believe it . . . Betty Grable's still married.

They announced that there will be nylon stockings again by Christmas. I won't say the women are anxious, but this is the first time Congress ever got fifty million letters petitioning it to abolish October and November.

And now that the war's over they're going to sell jeeps to the civilians . . . What a break for women . . . Now if they miss a pedestrian on the sidewalk . . . they can go right up the telephone pole after him.

They're already starting to build automobiles again . . . One factory went back into auto production so fast the first one came out with a Ninth Air Force pilot driving it.

And the automobile factories don't have to worry about salesmen anymore. The customers are so eager, they just come right in the factory and the workers build a car around them.

Now that the war is over, England needs money. When Truman met Winston Churchill he said to Winston, "You look like a million dollars." And Churchill replied, "That'll do for a down payment."

Churchill brought Truman a present all the way from England, and Harry wanted to give him something to take back, but Eisenhower wouldn't fit in his suitcase.

———

I T TOOK AWHILE getting back to being home, looking at people dressed in civvies. Soon after I returned, there was the famous 1948 presidential election, in which everyone expected Truman to lose to Dewey. The *Chicago Tribune* was so sure of it that their headline on election night read "Dewey Defeats Truman." When it was revealed the following morning that Truman had in fact been elected, I wrote a one-word congratulatory telegram to Truman in the White House: "Unpack." Harry kept that wire on his desk in the Oval Office.

———

The Democrats did so well in this election, they're even coming out with new products named after the president. They've got a thing now called the "Harry Truman Popsicle." It's a frozen Republican on a stick.

With the election out of the way, a lot of people had to change their plans. Now Margaret Truman has to go back to the White House. And she had it all set to be the fourth Andrews Sister.

The three candidates have really changed their tune since the elections. Truman's changed from "Missouri Waltz" to "It's Magic" . . . Dewey's humming "Say It Isn't So" . . . And Wallace is singing "On a Slow Boat to China."

———————

A FEW WEEKS BEFORE Christmas, I got a call from my friend Stuart Symington, who was Truman's secretary of the Air Force. He asked if I would headline a group that was going over to raise the spirits of the men and women of the Berlin Airlift. I managed to get Irving Berlin, Jinx Falkenberg with her husband Tex McCrary, a dozen Radio City Rockettes, my radio gang, plus Dolores.

———————

How do you do, everybody. This is Bob (here in Berlin to entertain the men in the airlift) Hope saying I'm here with Swan Soap in lots . . . meet me tonight in Potsdamer Platz.

As we arrived over Berlin several Soviet planes started to buzz us, but the first Russian pilot took one look at me and said, "They're okay, look at the hammerhead—and sickle."

And the people here really know me. Whenever I walk down the streets of Berlin, everybody follows me yelling and cheering. Any of you fellows know what Schweinehund means?

Just before we landed here we got the weather report. It was "Fog, followed by falling radio antennas."

Of course, weather reports around here are amazing . . . I heard one yesterday that went like this: Tempelhof, fog . . . Gatow, fog . . . Munich, fog . . . and Wiesbaden . . . er . . . ah . . . Wiesbaden . . . That's funny, Wiesbaden was here a minute ago.

And all this fog and bad visibility really keeps the boys flying low. In fact, one pilot was going over a farm yesterday and flew so low milk started forming on the wings . . . He was lucky the cow wasn't knock-kneed.

The good old Air Force hasn't changed, though . . . They make you spend an hour getting into a parachute, then fly so low you wouldn't have time to open an umbrella.

And is this Tempelhof Airdrome busy . . . There's so much air traffic in the sky around here, yesterday they found a pigeon living in a gopher hole.

We were up so high, I said to General Doolittle, "How near are we to Heaven?" He took one look at the gas gauge and said, "Nearer than you think."

I asked one pilot if he actually was facing death twice daily . . . He said, "No, . . . they've stopped serving Spam."

When we flew up the airlift corridor today the Russians were practicing ack-ack on both sides of it . . . Now I know what they mean by General Clay's pigeons.

Before we left the United States I learned to say, "Hi, neighbor," in French, Portuguese, Arabian, Indonesian, and South African Ubangi. We had a cockeyed pilot and we weren't sure where we'd land.

And Irving Berlin was on the plane with us . . . He didn't help our morale any . . . All the way across he kept singing, "How Deep Is the Ocean."

I thought the airlift planes were only equipped to bring in food, but General Clay said, "Don't worry, Bob, we've got a place for you." You know, nineteen and a half hours is a long time to hang from a meat hook . . . I didn't mind that so much . . . But the ham hock on the next hook kept sneering at me.

———

I TOOK MY FIRST plunge into TV in 1950. Frigidaire sponsored the special "Star Spangled Revue," which featured my guest stars Douglas Fairbanks Jr., Beatrice Lillie, and Dinah Shore.

I've been asked by a lot of people if there's much difference between working for TV and for radio. I honestly think that the secret of TV is to be relaxed, casual, and easy. I used to work very fast on the radio because I found out when I was working for service audiences, they wanted it fast. They didn't want situation comedy; they wanted jokes and they wanted them right now. I carried this technique into my first days on television, but I wasn't too successful. With that particular type of material and a civilian audience, I was ahead of them, and working too fast for them. I've slowed down for television, especially with my monologues.

The truth is that when you're right in the room with those who watch you and listen to you, as you are in TV, practically sitting in their laps and muttering into their ears, your personality is more important than anything you say.

Well, I've finally taken the plunge into TV. They asked me in such a way I couldn't refuse. They were using Kate Smith for a paperweight.

After I said yes, they put in the decimal point.

But I didn't just step into television. I had an audition. They gave me a tryout and I passed every test for television but one. In wrestling trunks I looked like Gorgeous George's mother.

The last time I was in New York, I worked for two weeks with Jane Russell and now I'm on for Frigidaire. Y'know, it's a great way to get pneumonia.

There's such a tremendous cast in this show they really had to rush to get all our makeup on. What a system! Five minutes before curtain time, they lined us all up in the hall and Helena Rubenstein skated by with a seltzer bottle full of Glo-coat.

Y'know, every comedian has his own particular way of telling a joke. I tell 'em fast . . . Ed Wynn tells 'em slow . . . Berle tells 'em a week late.

I wasn't sure television was here to stay, so I bought a very small set. It has a three-inch screen. You don't sit in front of it; you strap it over one eye.

Of course, you all know what television is. Remember vaudeville dying? Well, you're looking at the box they put it in.

I didn't want to rush into this thing. I wanted to find out first if television was just a fad. I've made wrong guesses before. Back in California I've got a chain of miniature golf courses, and a garage full of mah-jongg sets.

But it's a wonderful medium. Now you can not only see F. E. Boone. You can watch his tonsils sort out the tobacco.

This sight stuff is so much better than radio. Now when I lay an egg, I've got witnesses to prove I'm its mother.

I really like television, though. It's wonderful. You don't have to stand still in front of the microphone when you tell your jokes. You can move around. [Walking back and forth.] It's so much more casual . . . and relaxed . . . and safer.

I spent all day with the cameramen trying to figure out from which angle I look best. But the sponsor wanted you to see my face.

I like television so far, but my profile is causing some confusion. A guy in Indiana just ruined his screen trying to open a bottle of beer.

I ALSO WENT TO Korea—where our troops were stationed as peacekeepers—with another USO troupe in 1950. It was on this same trip that my gang was invited to lunch by General and Mrs. MacArthur. That was quite a treat.

I don't know how Truman and MacArthur feel about each other, but one left E. H. Waldorf just as the other one entered. That was three days ago and the revolving door is still spinning.

I was just in New York and it's still hard to get tickets to *South Pacific*. Of course, not as hard as it is for MacArthur to get tickets to America.

Here we are in Seoul, Korea . . . I never thought I'd get so far east I'd be homesick for Japan . . . Seoul has changed hands so many times the towels in the hotels are marked "His," "Hers," and "Who's occupying us now?"

I really didn't intend to perform so far north, but the first cavalry went through and the suction pulled me with them . . . And some of these towns are changing hands so fast, one soldier bought a lamp with three thousand yuan and got his change in rubles . . . But the way the war's going doesn't bother the Russians . . . They just run the newsreels backward and it looks like the North Koreans are advancing.

I asked a GI here how to tell a North Korean from a South Korean, and he said, "Turn your back" . . . I did and two blocks later I found out I had a set of twins strapped on my rumble seat . . . Just call me "Mamma San."

And there is a distinctive odor here . . . All I can tell you is my incense has been AWOL since Taejon . . . And I don't know what kind of germs they have here, but I walked by a pool of water today and my vaccination hissed at it . . . They've got germs over here that haven't been written up in *Reader's Digest* yet.

They have so much rice in Korea . . . After a wedding they throw the bride and groom at it.

BACK HOME, THE REPUBLICANS claimed the White House for the first time in twenty years with the election of Dwight D. Eisenhower. Most of America liked Ike.

After the swearing-in ceremonies, fifty thousand Republicans paraded through the streets of Washington for three hours . . . Nobody could remember how to get to the Capitol!

I don't blame Eisenhower for throwing out the silk hat tradition at his inauguration . . . He's the first Republican to be elected in twenty years and he had a right to *flip his lid*!!

You could tell which were the Republicans and which were the Democrats at the inauguration . . . The Republicans were facing the platform.

They had a lot of musical talent at the inauguration. And they wanted to invite José Iturbi, but Ike was against it. He said, "The last time we had a piano player in Washington, he stayed for eight years!"

When General Ike entered the White House, he immediately sent a message back to Republican headquarters. He wired, "Mission accomplished, our forces occupying objective, Democrats routed, no apparent resistance except for light sniper fire from the Steinway piano."

I wouldn't want to say the White House was booby-trapped, but the general's bed was short-sheeted . . . There was salt in the sugar bowl . . . And all the doors to the washroom were marked "Enlisted Personnel Only."

President Eisenhower is a great outdoorsman. He's the only man in the country who can start a fire by rubbing two Democrats together.

This is the first time I've seen him since I shook hands with him in Africa during the war . . . I guess he finally missed his ring!

———————

IN 1953, I WAS asked to host the Academy Awards again. This time was kind of special, because it was the first time the Oscars were televised.

———————

Good evening, ladies and gentlemen . . . I'm very glad to be here at the wedding of television and motion pictures . . . And just like many another Hollywood wedding . . . it's comforting to know that Las Vegas is so handy.

This event tonight marks the birth of a new era. The Academy Awards is the very own child of motion pictures, but I never expected them to entrust it to TV. That's like calling in a tiger for a baby-sitter.

This is the first time the Academy Awards have been on television; you see the faces of the winners and you see the faces of the losers congratulating the winners . . . Tonight you're gonna see some real Academy Award acting.

Television . . . That's where movies go when they die.

But television is wonderful. Now you can sit home and see Broadway shows, go to church in your living room . . . You don't have to go outside for anything . . . I was born on a farm . . . where you had to go outside for everything.

Paramount doesn't mind my doing television shows. In fact, they insist on it. I think that's a pretty sneaky way to cripple a new medium.

NONE OF US SUSPECTED, early on in the carefree
'50s, that something called the Cold War was
about to begin. We didn't even realize that the drive-
in hamburger joints, the neon Coke machines, the
over-chromiumed convertibles, the deafening music,
and the poodle skirts would one day be called "Amer-

icana" and be fondly revived in the '80s as symbols of the era of happy '50s innocence.

As I told one audience, "It's starting out to be a busy year for me. Between television, my daytime and nighttime radio shows, pictures, and personal appearances, I'm also working on a plan where, when you close your eyes, I appear on the inside of your eyelids."

Then I went on to world affairs.

I wanna say hello to one of our viewers who's never had a chance to watch me until now. Welcome, Joe DiMaggio! I was amazed when I heard that Joe had left Marilyn. I've heard of men giving up smoking, but this is ridiculous . . . it could set Wheaties back ten years.

But this meeting between Winnie and Ike is really top secret . . . It must be . . . they won't even let Roy Cohn in.

Churchill had to knock seven times before Ike would let him into the White House. He thought it was McCarthy.

Well, those Washington hearings finally came to an end. They had to . . . they ran out of generals.

Now that McCarthy's through investigating the Army, he's going to work on the biggest secret of all. Ike's golf score.

I enjoyed Eisenhower's "Be Calm" speech last week. And I know some of his calmness rubbed off on me because all through the speech I sat there calmly rocking back and forth . . . Of course, it would have been better if I'd been in a rocking chair.

Eisenhower assured us that Russia wouldn't attack . . . so I don't think the Army has anything to worry about because I don't believe McCarthy even has the H-bomb.

No wonder there's so much confusion in Washington . . . Everybody back there spends all their time under their desks . . . If they're not practicing for an H-bomb attack they're hiding from McCarthy.

I ALSO HAD A NEW movie to plug, *The Seven Little Foys*, with Jimmy Cagney. Jimmy was known as a tough guy in pictures, but he always said, "I'm a song-and-dance man." Believe me, he was a song-and-dance man in spades. Cagney and I danced a wonderful thank-you to the memory of the old-time vaudevillian Eddie Foy. That dance sequence helped make the film a huge hit.

———————

I've been busy over at Paramount, finishing my new picture, *The Seven Little Foys*. I work with a lot of kids in this picture. Theater screens are so wide nowadays, actors have to work in bunches.

Eddie Foy had so many kids he didn't know what to do with them, so he put them into his act . . . he was the Crosby of the Gaslight Era.

If you appear alone on those wide screens, you look like a nervous toothpick.

Paramount's done everything to make you like the picture. It's shot in VistaVision, Stereophonic

Sound, and Technicolor. If you're still not happy, I come to the theater and blow up your seat cushion.

ABOUT THIS SAME TIME, my autobiography was published. First, it was serialized in the *Saturday Evening Post* and then it was released as a book called *Have Tux, Will Travel*. The title is one from my old vaudeville days. Actors used to say on their cards or in ads, "Have Tuxedo, Will Travel." Talk about seeing your life flash before your eyes. Little did I know that book, written in the '50s, would cover only half my life.

Incidentally, I can't say enough to you people who went in and bought copies of my book, *Have Tux, Will Travel* . . . And I'd like to say plenty to you people who didn't.

You'll like this book. It starts out by telling all my good points, all my achievements, and gives the entire history of my education . . . The second page is good, too.

You could buy my book in a paperback edition for a dollar, and in hard covers for $3.50. And for fifty cents extra, I come around to your house personally and wet your finger while you're turning the pages.

Jack Benny really liked my book. I know because he called me up from the library and told me.

My book is really exciting. It tells the story of a poor, barefoot boy in Cleveland who was determined to be a comedian regardless of his talent.

———————

IN 1956, EISENHOWER WAS at the peak of his popularity, so his rematch with Adlai Stevenson was rather lopsided. Ike won by an electoral vote of 457 to 73. The campaign was as exciting as sitting around watching concrete harden. The only humorous highlight came from Stevenson's running mate, Tennessee senator Estes Kefauver, who insisted on wearing a coonskin cap throughout the campaign.

———————

If Kefauver is elected, it'll be interesting. I just can't wait to see the White House done over in coonskin.

That feud between Kefauver and Stevenson made headlines, but outside of politics they're actually very good friends. For instance, the other night Stevenson couldn't sleep, so Kefauver sent him a sleeping pill. It weighed four pounds.

I joke about the candidates, but it's all in fun. I'd be in an awful spot if I came out for one candidate and the other side won . . . Wouldn't I look great picking grapes?

I stay right in the middle of the road . . . Like a California driver.

Ike is all Army. He loves golf, but if you lose, you not only have to pay him, he makes you eat K-rations. And sometimes, Ike cooks. I once played nine holes with one of his meatballs.

Mamie is really relieved that Ike has another four years in the White House. She hadn't had time to clean up the spike marks in the hallway.

The inauguration was televised and one Democrat was complaining about it. He said, "That's the trouble with television—too many reruns."

The guests at the inaugural dinner consumed a terrific amount of food—3,000 steaks, 1,000 hamburgers, 200 turkeys . . . and Lawrence Welk's drummer is missing.

Did you see President Eisenhower's press conference on TV? I thought Ike was very good, although he could use a little coaching. A couple of times there he was smiling at Democrats.

The president's press conference got a wonderful review in *Variety*. It said, "Prez Smash at News Bash. Ike No Rube on Tube."

Ike is really quite a good painter. In fact, I hear that every time he goes out to play golf, Grandma Moses heaves a sigh of relief.

I think it's wonderful that Ike paints; it's relaxing, and besides, a guy without a steady job should always have something to fall back on.

B ECAUSE WE WERE in the middle of the Cold War, I really wanted to get to Russia to try and figure out what made them tick, no pun intended. After a lot of "Red Tape" and runaround, I was finally cleared to land in Moscow. I had brought along a small crew with the idea of filming part of the trip to include in a television special.

I also hired a Russian cameraman, who filmed my monologue from Spasso House. We tried to get as many English-speaking people as we could, so that the jokes would play. The American ambassador, Llewellyn Thompson, was a big help in getting me an audience.

———————

It's very exciting to be here in Moscow with you Democrats . . . you must be Democrats or you wouldn't be here.

I hope you'll be cooperative tonight. On my passport I wrote "Comedian" and I'd hate to have the Russians think I lied.

The State Department was glad to let me come here. I'm cooperative, I'm personable, and I'm charming and expendable.

But it's really a thrill to be in Russia. I know I'm in Russia . . . this morning my stomach got up two hours before I did and had a bowl of borscht.

How about that vodka. Now I know why they got their sputnik up first . . . I'm surprised the whole country isn't up there with it.

The Russians are overjoyed with their sputnik. It's kind of weird being in a country where every ninety minutes there's a national holiday . . . anybody without a stiff neck is a traitor . . . it's the big topic of conversation everyplace but the dog show.

It's pretty nervous staying in a country where the government owns everything. If you steal a towel, it's a federal rap. I've had to unpack three times.

But it's amazing the way people can get the wrong impression. One Russian official showed me a picture of the starving people in America. People without shoes and nothing to eat, absolutely desperate. And I couldn't argue with him . . . it was a picture of the bus station in Las Vegas.

———————

WHENEVER I'D ENTER my room, I'd pound on the wall and yell, "Testing! Testing! One! Two! Three! Am I coming in loud and clear?" And whenever we were discussing anything that might in any way be misinterpreted, one of us would look up the ventilator and holler, "Only kidding, Kru!" We were actually half-joking when we did this, but it was a joke only because there was a possibility that the Big Bear was listening.

Jack Benny asked me to bring back a fur hat with a part in it. So I crossed Red Square to visit the GUM department store.

———————

Don't let anyone tell you that the Russians aren't passionate. At the perfume counter they displayed such sexy-sounding scents as "Kremlin" and "Our Moscow." I don't know how they missed "Moonlight on the Collective Farm," "Volga Boatman," and "Essence of Tractor." This one not only smells good, but it's wonderful for lubricating a fan belt. Instead of "My Sin" it's "Where Do I Go to Confess?"

———————

I HAD A LOT OF tense moments in Russia, like the time I returned to my hotel to find my room ransacked and my stuff—including my jokes—strewn all over the place. While I found the experience of being in enemy territory fascinating, I was happy when I returned to the good ole USA.

Soon, however, I was off again to do what would become an annual Hope tradition, a Christmas show overseas. This time, Thule, Greenland, was selected because the Cold War was heating up and Thule was an early warning station. Our plane landed in sub-zero weather and it was dark. Of course, it was dark twenty-four hours a day during the winter.

———————

I'm very happy to be here in Thule. The temperature is thirty-six below. Only, we don't know below what . . . the thermometer went AWOL.

The guys get pretty lonesome up here. When a wolf howls he starts a community sing. It's so lonely here, one guy is going steady with his tattoo . . . and his friends keep asking him if she's got a sister.

You're not even allowed to think about girls up here. At night a sergeant walks through the barracks and wakes up anybody with a smile on his face.

IN 1957, THE U.S. suddenly had to give up its belief that the Russian scientists were just a Polish joke. *Sputnik 1* beeped its way around the world 560 miles above the earth and sent a couple million American schoolkids back to arithmetic class. The USSR had gotten an "A" in science. The Space Age had dawned, and it had a Russian accent.

The space race was on. In Washington, people were deciding what to do since Eisenhower couldn't run again. Was it going to be Nixon or an almost unknown senator from Massachusetts, John Fitzgerald Kennedy? The televised debates made all the difference.

One nice thing about the debates . . . the one who loses can prove to the unemployment office that he really *tried* to get a job!

Did you see Nixon and Kennedy on TV . . . in the hour version of *To Tell the Truth*?

I love the way the southern papers listed the great debate . . . "two Yankees chewin' the fat."

Those debates are exciting . . . but I'll be glad when it's over. I hate long commercials.

I keep waiting for the moderator to say, "Will the real president step forward."

Things are pretty rough when the presidency of the United States hangs on a makeup man's sponge.

The campaign really is getting rough, you know. The other night while Kennedy was speaking, Nixon stood behind him humming "Rag Mop."

They both promised to help the farmers . . . And they sure did. An hour of that would help *any* crop!

Max Factor just came out with a new makeup for candidates—"Instant Honest."

Kennedy looked a little nervous. He'd never been allowed to stay up that late before.

Did you see the great debate between Nixon and Kennedy last week? It was listed in *TV Guide* as "Youth wants you to know."

———————

WHILE SOME OF the country was listening to the television debates, the beatniks were presenting a face that was unfamiliar to most Americans. Rock 'n' roll was in and so was a handsome young singer from Memphis who, with his sideburns, tight pants, and guitar, turned popular music on its ear.

———————

A beatnik is someone who bathes regularly in the La Brea tar pits.

They wear old clothes . . . They hate to work . . . And they never have any money. We used to have the same thing in Cleveland. We called 'em relatives.

My cousin wanted to be a beatnik, but they threw him out. They caught him looking happy.

They're very different from the rest of us. A beatnik is a guy who gets up in the morning, goes over to the window, and looks in.

They sit around coffeehouses and they're very talented . . . artists, writers, poets, sculptors, shipping clerks. . . . Someone's gotta pay the check.

And they're very literary. One beatnik refuses to eat breakfast. Because the directions on the Wheaties box weren't written by T. S. Eliot.

Beatniks are really unconventional. In fact, one beatnik was thrown out of a coffeehouse because his poem rhymed.

They think a little different from the rest of us. A beatnik is a guy who gets up in the morning, looks out at the sunshine, takes a deep breath of fresh air, and says, "I wish I were dead."

Elvis is just a young, clean-cut American boy who does in public what everybody else does in private.

I love the way he sings . . . but if he ever gets rid of the hiccups, he's out of business.

Do I sound like I'm jealous of Elvis? . . . I am—his teddy bear gets more fan mail than I do.

But you've gotta hand it to this kid. A few months ago he couldn't spell Tennessee . . . now he owns it.

And you know those long sideburns of his? They're there for a reason. They cover up his earplugs . . . He can't stand his singing either.

And rock and roll is catching on all over . . . France . . . England . . . They even have it in Japan, only over there they call it judo.

The idea is to rock your hips and roll your shoulders . . . The dance was originated by Crosby . . . He got the idea one morning while he was trying to get into his girdle.

I attended one rock and roll session at the Palladium . . . I was very lucky, I came home with my own hips.

I N NOVEMBER OF 1960, Kennedy won the presidential election by .3 percent. And seemingly, before the last vote was counted, he had presented the names for his young Cabinet, including his brother Bobby as attorney general. I shared the dais with JFK at the Alfalfa Club dinner in February 1961, and couldn't resist . . .

Here I am, starting another season in television. What else can I do? I'm too old to be a candidate . . . A few months ago Kennedy's mother said, "You have a choice. Do you want to go to camp this year or run for president?"

President Kennedy has picked pretty good help— Harvard is emptier than our Treasury. There are so many professors in the Cabinet that you can't leave the White House without raising your hand . . . The attorney general was twenty minutes late for a meeting this morning and he had to bring a note from his mother.

I like giving youth a chance, but do we really want a president who rides for half fare on the bus?

———

DURING HIS TURN at the podium, Kennedy feigned surprise that anyone would object to his nominating his brother as attorney general: "What's wrong with his getting a little legal experience before he goes into business for himself?" What set Kennedy apart from all other presidents before him was his ability to genuinely laugh at himself. He opened the floodgates for presidential humor, the likes of which had never been seen before. He enjoyed the ribbing and gave as good as he got. He could ad-lib with you on equal terms. Not just with me, but everybody. No topic seemed sacred—his family, his rocking chair, his foreign policy.

———

A few months ago, who'd have thought Ike would be a full general again and Kennedy would be singing "That Old Rockin' Chair's Got Me."

Wasn't that a wonderful meeting at the White House between Eisenhower and Kennedy?

Eisenhower said, "Congratulations on your victory," and Kennedy replied, "I had to win. It's so tough these days to find a place that'll take children."

Have you heard about President Kennedy's new youth Peace Corps to help foreign countries? It's sort of *Exodus* with fraternity pins.

And that Kennedy's press conferences were being beamed to Russia? . . . The Russians love the show—they've added a laugh track.

And what about Kennedy asking for two and a half billion more for his budget? He hasn't thrown out Ike's old budget—he's using it for petty cash.

We expected some breakage in the White House, but that Caroline is too much.

THERE WERE SOME MAJOR problems for the Kennedy "New Frontier" program that became a challenge for comedy. First was the Bay of Pigs, then there was Vietnam, trouble in Laos, and a slight recession—and we were lagging in space. But laughter prevailed.

Somehow with the low points there was always a flip side. The Kennedy family and their activities always made good copy: Jacqueline wearing a short designer dress to church; JFK inviting cellist Pablo Casals to entertain "at home"; playing touch football on the White House lawn, or taking fifty-mile hikes; and brother Teddy running for senator of Massachusetts.

––––––––––

It's been a very depressing month. We're still behind in the space race, there's trouble in China, Laos, and Vietnam. Right about now, Mr. Nixon must get the feeling he won.

Things are so bad that last week Huntley tried to jump off Brinkley.

Really, I don't envy President Kennedy. For the first time I'm worried if he has enough hair to last out the job.

It's been a slow year back home—only one Kennedy got elected.

The Kennedys had a nice Christmas: Jackie got a new pair of water skis, the president got a pair of hair clippers, and Ted got a nice present—Massachusetts.

There was a wonderful Christmas spirit in Washington this year. The Kennedys held a drive to raise money to buy toys for needy Republicans.

I don't blame Jacqueline Kennedy, who gave a TV tour of the White House, for going on television. Look what it did for her husband.

The president's wife just returned from a shopping trip around the world. It wasn't too successful. She couldn't decide which country to buy.

Isn't she beautiful? She's a wonderful answer to all this talk about the ugly American. I think we should put her in the State Department. She visited two countries and didn't have to duck once.

Her trip was sponsored by the International Association of World Peace, the International Committee for Refugee Child Welfare, and *Vogue* magazine.

IN SEPTEMBER 1962, President Kennedy presented me with the Congressional Gold Medal in the Rose Garden of the White House. I thanked him for the honor and said "Mr. President, I feel very humble, but I think I have the strength of character to fight it."

The baseball season opened this month. In Washington, President Kennedy threw out the first ball. He threw it at the president of U.S. Steel.

The White House press conference proved that the prez really has got a temper. The cherry trees blossomed three weeks earlier this year. I hate to think what'll happen if the price of haircuts ever goes up.

Kennedy was so mad he called the Cabinet, the Joint Chiefs of Staff, all his brothers and had the Atlantic fleet anchor off Pittsburgh.

And I don't think it helped when the president of U.S. Steel, Roger Blough, visited the White House wearing his "I like Ike" button.

And I wanna tell you one thing: they better not push Kennedy too hard. One of these days, he might give up the presidency and go back into money.

You know, when the Russian cosmonauts landed, Khrushchev kissed them. When our astronauts land, President Kennedy only shakes their hands. We may be behind in the space race, but at least we know what we're whistling at.

I guess you heard. The president suggested we join with the Russians to go to the moon. And Khrushchev was delighted. He said, "Today the moon, tomorrow Disneyland."

I just got back from Washington. I flew back. It was a little too far to walk. That walking bit is part of President Kennedy's physical fitness program. He's trying to get the country back on its feet.

What a family. When they're not running for something, they're walking.

No, Mrs. Kennedy said they were looking for paintings of authentic American history, like Crosby with

his first son . . . Uncle Miltie [Berle] in a Paris gown
. . . Zsa Zsa Gabor joining the PTA.

Maybe Kennedy's younger than we think. Milk—is
he really Irish?

You all heard that President Kennedy will be
visiting Palm Springs next week. He had to come—
it's the only place a member of his family hasn't visited this month. He's visiting all the underdeveloped
areas. Some of the houses there still don't have their
own golf courses.

The president is flying to California, his wife is
shopping in Italy and India, and Bobby is traveling
to Japan. Remember the good ol' days when you
knew where the president was? On the golf course.

President Kennedy is just winding up a nonpolitical
tour of the eleven states he lost in the last election.
He wanted to see how they're getting along without
federal aid.

Bobby Kennedy is really in good shape; he went
fifty miles. Imagine what he would do with [union
leader] Jimmy Hoffa off his back.

I guess the president wasn't kidding when he said we must proceed with "viga."

THE LAST THING Kennedy said to me was "The next time you're in town, bring your sticks . . . we'll go out and knock it." He loved competitive sports just as he loved the competitiveness of politics. He played everything to win.

Just a few days after Kennedy's assassination, I had to have eye surgery, and the doctors warned me that I needed to cut back on my schedule. I took a few weeks off to rest and promised our band of gypsies that I would catch up with them in Turkey for our annual Christmas junket. I left to meet them, with everyone from Dolores to the doctors thinking I was crazy. Actually, I felt better and better the more laughs I got. Laughter really is the best medicine.

I almost didn't make this trip because of a clot in my left eye. They thought it might affect the brain, but they examined it and found nothing.

I think it was a GI doctor. He didn't examine my eyes, he just counted 'em.

They didn't use an anesthetic . . . they didn't have to . . . when I heard I was going to the hospital, I fainted.

I just got the bill from my doctors. Now I know what they mean by "an eye for an eye."

I just had my eye checked. I said, "Doctor, will I be able to play golf again?" He said, "Certainly" . . . which is good news because I never could before.

I was in the hospital for five days with my eyes under wraps . . . I had to operate mostly by feel . . . There . . . that oughta explain it to those stuck-up nurses.

The doctor warned me to take it easy. He said, "Remember, Mr. Hope, when a man gets to be forty, these things take a while. Just think how long it's going to take you."

Seriously, they don't even want me to have exciting dreams. And since I've been eating in the mess hall here, I haven't.

A FTER THE DEATH of Kennedy, Lyndon Baines Johnson was sworn in as president. He finished out the last year or so of Kennedy's term and then ran for the top job himself. It was kind of a good news–bad news situation for him. The good news, he was president; the bad news, it was the turbulent

'60s, the conflict in Vietnam was escalating, and so was opposition to the war.

Johnson was in top form in 1964 when I was in D.C. to receive the USO Silver Medal. Although he wasn't thought of as much of a joke-teller, LBJ gave a hilarious speech in my honor—the audience was responding to him like *he* was one of the nation's top comics. He was a tough act to follow, but I tried . . .

––––––––––

Thank you very much, Mr. President. [To the audience] Wasn't that a crazy drop-in? An extra chair turned up fast, didn't it?

It's nice to be back here in Washington. Or, as the Republicans call it, Camp Runamuck . . . No, but it's nice to be back here in Birdland.

I want you to know that this material was written without the knowledge that you [Johnson] were going to be here. I have to do it, it's here on the paper.

When we get the "Great Society," there'll be no more pain, no tension, no headaches, no stomach acid, and no tired blood. It may be good for the country, but it's gonna take all the fun out of commercials.

No one's figured out where we're going to get the money for all this. Maybe he's gonna put the entire country on the Diners Club card.

Yessir, the prez says he's gonna increase federal benefits, lower taxes, have Medicare for pets, and we're all gonna be rich—I just wonder under which shell he hid the pea.

———

JOHNSON DECLARES WAR on Poverty—"Lights out." When the prez found out the electric light bill at the White House was running three thousand dollars a month, he turned out all the lights. Now, it's running three thousand a month for broken legs.

———

I was invited to stay at the White House, but I didn't have a flashlight with me.

Lynda Bird just signed with *McCall's* magazine as a writer and youth consultant. And you thought the president was kidding about his War on Poverty.

I think Lynda Bird deserves a lot of credit for working. She could have gone into politics.

Johnson's proposed national budget, $196 billion: It was a typical Texan's budget. It balances perfectly providing they strike oil under the White House.

Of course, no one knows what the president has in the back of his mind. He may be thinking of selling something—like Michigan.

One item in the budget is $50 million to fight crime. There's only one way to wipe out crime in this country. Put a tax on it. If it's high enough, nobody could afford to steal.

PRESIDENT JOHNSON, LIKE ALL presidents, enjoyed a honeymoon period, while the country did a bit of healing. The Beatles were a distraction for the teenagers as well as the rest of us. There was a popular show called *Mr. Ed*, about a talking horse, and on television we had Beatles that could sing.

Talking horses, singing Beatles . . . Ed Sullivan just scratched himself and found a new act.

First it was the "Crickets," now the "Beatles." I saw a spider this morning and I was afraid to step on it . . . he might be a star.

The Crickets, the Beatles . . . at least it answers the question where our new talent is coming from . . . under the kitchen sink.

The Beatles are kind of a barbershop quartet that couldn't get waited on.

I see that the Beatles have arrived by plane from England. They were forty pounds overweight and that was just their hair.

How about those Beatles from England? Won't they ever forgive us for the Boston Tea Party?

———————

IN 1965, THE Defense Department sent me and my troupe to Vietnam. Our exact destination was kept secret, even from us, as I was deemed a prime target for the Vietcong. The first location turned out to be Bien Hoa, on the outskirts of Saigon. Twenty-three thousand armed GIs were waiting for us when we stepped on the stage.

———————

Here I am in Bien Hoa. That's Vietnamese for "duck."

Nice to be here in Sniper Valley.

You remember Vietnam . . . it's that place Huntley and Brinkley are always talking about.

We're going to Saigon and I hope I do as well here as Henry Cabot Lodge . . . he got out.

What a welcome I got at the airport . . . they thought I was a replacement.

And as we flew in today, they gave us a twenty-one-gun salute . . . three of them were ours.

I understand the enemy is very close. But with my act, they always are.

No, we're happy to be here. You know, I asked Secretary McNamara if we could come here, and he said, "Why not? We've tried everything else."

This is a terrible country for a coward. Can you imagine my not knowing which way to run? You've heard of the NBC peacock. This is the Far Eastern chicken.

What a welcome! Wherever we go, we're met by thousands of cheering servicemen. They think I'm Secretary McNamara with the shutdown orders . . . one of the bases they closed so fast, they had to reopen to get me out. I was stuck in the nurses' quarters and who needed help?

———

I WANT YOU TO know our Christmas show had the highest rating in television, and I'd feel very happy about it, except for the fact that it took the bombing of our hotel in Saigon to do it . . . One reason for the tremendous audience was that my life was really in danger. Which only proves one thing: to get a rating, give the public what they want.

———

WHEN WE GOT BACK home, we found that the growing casualty lists and the televised news from the battlefronts were having a tremendous effect on popular opinion, especially in the colleges, where political protests usually start—as we had seen recently in China, East Germany, and Czechoslovakia. In addition to demonstrating, students were burning their draft cards, letting their hair grow long . . .

Have you seen some of the hairdos the kids are wearing? One kid's sideburns were so long he had to cut armholes in them.

How about men wearing their hair long? The newest thing is the sheepdog look. That's true . . . I know one woman who walks her husband every morning.

Things surely have changed. I walked in the barbershop the other day, and there were four guys sitting under the hair dryer discussing the Dodgers.

I don't have much news from back home. The student demonstrators have calmed down. They ran out of matches!

Colleges sure have changed. Today, the three "R"s are reading, 'riting, and rioting.

And how about that new draft lottery? It started a whole new thing. Yesterday, seventeen students burned their birth certificates.

What a way to celebrate your birthday . . . they give you a big cake and a girl jumps out of it with your induction notice.

Who wants to hear a happy birthday telegram sung by a sergeant.

I called the draft board and asked what my number was. They said, "For what war?"

Did you hear where they may cut out the draft? The new army is going to be made up entirely of volunteers . . . he arrives Friday.

Congress would like to outlaw the draft completely. Remember when you felt the same way . . . before they got you? Now you'd like to see LBJ in!

They shouldn't have too much trouble getting volunteers . . . They just made a deal with *Playboy* to do the recruiting posters.

Say, have you been reading about the hippies? They just had a "love-in" in Los Angeles. You know what a "love-in" is? That's sort of an Italian movie—live!

You know what a hippie is? That's a girl with a nice figure that's gone to pot!

Have you seen a hippie group? It looks like a rummage sale with live rummage!

The fellows wear beads and earrings and the girls wear boots and blankets. The police don't know who to arrest for doing what to whom.

And that LSD is pretty powerful. One guy took some, tried to throw himself on the floor, and missed!

This is a tough problem. If we're not careful, this whole generation may go to pot.

A lot of them smoke those Tijuana Marlboros. Three drags and you're up in Dean Martin country.

For nine years, I kept going back to Vietnam and to the men and women who did their duty no matter the cost, and it used to tear me up to see kids back home protesting and trashing the memory of those who sacrificed so much. Nineteen sixty-eight was an especially tough year. Right after we returned home the Tet offensive began, and it was also the year that Martin Luther King and Bobby Kennedy were assassinated.

Nixon was running for the Republican nomination and people thought LBJ would go for a second term despite the protests. But he surprised everyone by deciding not to run. I was sorry to hear his decision because he was one tough guy and a man I respected. Throughout his presidency, I had a lot of fun with him.

When Charles de Gaulle got upset about the devaluation of the British pound, he wired Lyndon, "Lower your dollar." Johnson wired back, "Up your francs."

LBJ and Bobby Kennedy are very good friends. They lunched together only yesterday. LBJ picked up the check . . . and Bobby paid the food taster.

Can you imagine a Texan having a conversation with a New Englander? I wonder who the interpreter was.

They really can't agree on anything. You know how LBJ turns out all the lights in the White House? Guess who sneaks around and turns them back on?

Bobby phoned LBJ in Texas and said he wasn't the least bit interested in the White House. What LBJ didn't like about it was that Bobby was speaking from the Oval Office at the time.

President Johnson was in Palm Springs this weekend. I say if you're gonna fight poverty, go to the source.

The president is making a six-nation tour of Asia . . . he is traveling throughout the Far East to make friends. If it works, he may try it in this country.

He's going to visit all our allies over there. He may be back the same day.

There was one tense moment at the airport when leaving Washington. Vice President Humphrey held out his hand for the keys to the White House. LBJ finally handed them over, but he said, "Remember, I've still got the Army, Navy, and Texas."

How about President Johnson meeting with Vietnam's General Ky in Hawaii? They've made a decision about Vietnam that should please everybody—they're going to close it down.

The prez is really an amazing man. What other guy would plan a trip to exotic, romantic Hawaii and take Dean Rusk [secretary of state] with him?

The president loves Hawaii. Nobody has the heart to tell him it's not part of Texas.

However, the president was pretty upset en route to Hawaii. The in-flight movie starred Ronald Reagan.

I'm happy to report that the president is recovering nicely from his gallbladder surgery. Now we all know why he was so anxious for Medicare.

The operation was delayed for forty-eight hours while they found a surgeon who wasn't sore about Medicare.

It wasn't an easy operation for the surgeons. The president wouldn't let them turn the lights on.

Lyndon and Lady Bird will be returning to Texas but nothing will change much. Having herds of cattle is a lot like politics—you have to watch your step.

WHEN I RETURNED from yet another Christmas in Vietnam, lots was happening. There were student protests, continued peace talks in Paris, and Onassis married Jacqueline Kennedy.

How about that rich Greek winning the Irish Sweep-stakes? I never thought Carmen would be replaced by Toora Loora Loora.

Onassis is a very handsome man but he's only five foot four . . . twelve foot eight when he's standing on his money.

In fact, his bank refers to him as "The Jolly Greek Giant!"

He's a very successful man. At sixty-two, Onassis has more money than he can spend, more ships than he can sail, and Jackie.

Onassis is the world's richest ship owner. He owns a fleet of two hundred oil tankers . . . and that's just in his bathtub.

The honeymoon began on Monday. You know those Greeks . . . never on Sunday.

They're honeymooning on his yacht. Have you seen it? That's what the *Queen Mary* would look like if England had his money.

NIXON WON THE VOTE by a very narrow margin. I covered it on my TV special the day after the election.

Well, it's over, and from force of habit Nixon has just conceded.

I could tell Nixon was nervous—he was giving the victory sign with one finger. It was the closest election in history. The lead changed hands faster than a fan dancer working in the round.

But it was hardest on Spiro Agnew. Just when he was getting known, he becomes the vice president.

AND THERE WAS some good news for our space program. Neil Armstrong is what America is all about. He gave us something to be proud of during a really low point in America's history. And another of our astronauts, Alan Shepard, did a lot to warm the hearts of golfers everywhere.

Neil Armstrong is now the greatest man ever to come out of Ohio. Modesty prevents me from telling you who he replaced.

Neil is my idea of a real hero. He had a choice and he came back to this world.

Can you imagine being able to say that you left your footprints on the moon? I thought it was pretty wild when Tony Bennett left his heart in San Francisco.

How about Alan Shepard swinging that six-iron at the Fra Maura Country Club? Mission control was very upset . . . Their computers showed an eight-iron would have been enough.

And the nice thing about playing golf up there . . . you don't have to replace your divots.

What distance you get . . . Alan just tapped the ball and it disappeared over the horizon like Timothy Leary on his way to an acid bust.

Shepard's drive went over 900 yards . . . I finally figured out what's been holding my game back . . . Gravity.

The ball went farther than Shepard did on his first flight.

Nine hundred yards! I generally hit three shots in that distance. Spiro Agnew generally hits three people in that distance.

Nixon's chopper dropped him off in my backyard for a quick round of golf at nearby Lakeside.

I suppose you read where President Nixon stopped by and changed his clothes at my house . . . which is now officially designated as the Richard Nixon Memorial Locker Room.

I guess the president is worrying about 1972. Why else would he be going house to house? But that's the way it is with Republicans. Two weeks ago I had dinner at the White House, and Saturday I look up and there's the president on my doorstep.

Of course, it made me a big man on my block. From now on the sightseeing bus won't consider me just another rest stop.

I don't mean to call President Nixon a pigeon. That would be disrespectful. I won't even say who won the loot . . . but if you look through the president's $200 billion budget, I'm in there somewhere!

He's been practicing eating with chopsticks for his pending visit to China. He hasn't got anything in his mouth yet, but he's started two fires.

Nixon is a real expert on China. He can order without a menu.

Nixon's trip [to China] was an international success. A new poll shows that he has a better-than-ever chance of being reelected president of this country, and a 40 percent chance of being elected president of China.

Some conservatives feared Mr. Nixon lost his shirt in China, but that's not true. Kissinger found the laundry ticket and he's going back for it.

The Russians blasted Nixon's trip to China. They said the whole thing was to get Nixon reelected. I think that's kinda silly. How many Red Chinese are registered Republicans?

NIXON WON THE 1972 election by a landslide, defeating the Democratic ticket of George McGovern (senator from South Dakota) and R. Sargent Shriver Jr. One of his first acts was to change his Cabinet. Nixon asked everybody to send in their resignation.

The Nixon "V" sign we thought meant "victory." To the Cabinet, it meant "*vaya con Dios.*"

It really upset his wife, Pat. She thought the job was steady.

It's a strange sight at the unemployment office— the Nixon Cabinet standing behind George McGovern.

Did you see the pictures in the papers of President Nixon shopping in New York? I knew he was looking for a new Cabinet . . . but in Hammacher Schlemmer???

But I think Dr. Kissinger will be staying on. It's not easy to find a doctor who makes house calls all over the world.

———————

THE INVESTIGATION OF the 1972 Watergate break-in implicated Republican party officials, and Spiro Agnew resigned under pressure, pleading no contest to charges of income-tax evasion. House Minority Leader Gerald Ford replaced him as vice president. Nixon resigned from office on August 9, 1974. A friend was in trouble, and there was little to joke about and laugh at.

———————

Watergate proved to the country how tough it is to find good plumbers today. Here I am on my first show of the season and I want to thank the Watergate Committee for making room for me.

It appears that the president taped all his conversations in the Oval Office. I just hope that eighteen minutes of missing tape included some of the bad jokes I told him.

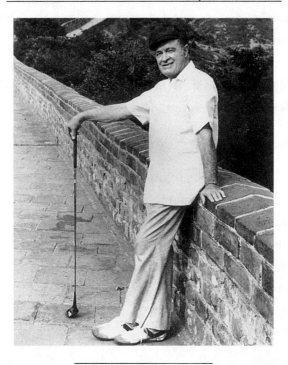

IF YOU WERE paying attention, you may remember that the Vietnam War finally ended in an agreement neither side intended to honor. It was like one of Zsa Zsa's weddings.

Gerald Rudolph Ford became the thirty-eighth president of the United States. Assuming the presidency following Nixon's resignation was not an easy task. The chair in the Oval Office was a hot seat. There were economic difficulties, and the Democrat-controlled Congress resisted his domestic and foreign initiatives and even gave him a bad time by delaying approval of his choice of Nelson Rockefeller for vice president. But I had a ball.

Ford is very down-to-earth. He's been president nearly two months now, and he still swims in the White House pool. Not once has he tried to walk across it. He's a real American. And if he keeps up the good work, he could be in the next Coke commercial.

I played golf with him a few times before he became president—when I still had a chance of winning.

Congress is sure taking its time to confirm Rockefeller. If they don't move fast, a lot of their credit cards will be canceled.

I hope Rocky is confirmed. It's what we've always needed: a politician who pays more taxes than we do. And a lot of people are surprised at Ford picking Rocky because, after all, Rocky's been trying to get the job of president for twelve years. That's like asking Morris the cat to watch your tuna sandwich.

They're getting ready for Yuletide at the White House. This morning, two wise men appeared on the lawn—there used to be three, but you know how Ford's been cutting down.

But it's thrilling to hear, in the middle of the recession, that someone got a job, especially such a deserving case as Nelson Rockefeller . . . doesn't it give you a warm feeling to know we're living in a country where any multimillionaire can become vice president?

With Rocky as vice president, it takes a load off the president's shoulders. Now he doesn't have to worry about meeting the national debt. He just slips it under Rocky's phone bill and lets it go at that.

———————

SHORTLY AFTER FORD assumed the presidency, he pardoned his former boss. He claimed that he did it to save the country from being divided one more time. Unfortunately, people still talked. And the leader of the Teamsters, Jimmy Hoffa, disappeared mysteriously. Sometimes they talked about things other than politics.

I don't think Hoffa's missing at all. I think he's just playing a game of hide-and-seek with Howard Hughes.

Those Teamsters are tough when you don't pay your dues.

He's from Detroit. He could have been recalled by Ralph Nader.

The police have flooded the country with Hoffa's description, "Short, tough, stocky, and loud." Totie Fields is afraid to leave the house.

There are all sorts of theories and some of them are ridiculous. I don't think Earl Butz sold him to Russia with the last wheat shipment.

Ford encouraged the country to celebrate the Bicentennial in a big way. I think he felt it would be an opportunity for the nation to come together and celebrate the land we love. Just about every city planned a special observance for the occasion.

Well, here it is, the Fourth of July, the big one . . . Two hundred years ago today we broke away from England and started driving on the other side of the road.

Some people put us down. But I still haven't heard of any Americans trying to swim across the border into Mexico!

And what abundance! What other country has five McDonald's for every two people?

And we lead the world in science and technology. Just think, in two hundred years, we've come up with Roto-Rooters, Glad bags, five-day deodorant pads . . . and margarine that talks back!

And our agriculture is the wonder of the world. Who else could send millions of tons of wheat to Russia and still have enough left for 80 million Twinkies?

———————

IT WAS NOT *President* Jerry Ford I got to know and like so well. It is "former president" Ford who has become such a good friend. It is Ford the golfer and Ford the joke maker, and his wife, Betty, who Dolores and I enjoy spending time with.

———————

The whole Ford family, Betty and the children, Susan, Jack, Mike, and Steve, are out campaigning for Jerry [against Jimmy Carter]. They're so all-American, every time I see them together I get the feeling they're going to do an orange juice commercial.

How about Betty Ford calling people in New Hampshire hoping to get their vote? It's kind of like Dial-A-Prayer in reverse. So that's why they asked me to pay my taxes in dimes.

They used to try to get the uncommitted vote. Now they try to get the unlisted.

It's been said that "behind every great man is a woman." For Betty Ford, that's a double blessing. The way Jerry plays golf, that's the safest place to be.

After Carter won the election, he celebrated with a champagne victory dinner . . . Ford split a "Big Mac" with Ronald Reagan.

President Ford is such a football fan, he's not calling himself a loser. For the next two months, he's just another free agent.

I knew that Carter lost California. When I woke up Wednesday, it was snowing in Los Angeles . . . but only on Republicans.

Ronald Reagan called Ford on Wednesday and said he was ready to campaign for him . . . that's what happens when you forget to set your clock back one hour.

Carter's already started to plan the White House transition. He's canceled their subscription to

Playboy . . . and replaced it with the *Farmer's Almanac.*

Ford offered to help Carter with the White House transition. Carter just told him to leave the keys with the neighbors.

In the next few weeks, we'll be hearing all about Miss Lillian, brother Billy, and daughter Amy . . . and I'm still having trouble trying to figure out which is Donny and which is Marie.

And Carter's already planning for his Inaugural Ball. For the first time in history, it won't be black tie . . . it'll be black-eyed peas and chitlins!

———————

THE CARTERS MOVED into the White House, and Jerry and Betty moved to Palm Springs. I was happy because I had a chance to get even on the golf course. All of us in Palm Springs are thrilled that the Fords moved there. And Betty is the envy of every housewife in the area. Who else could tell an ex-president to take out the garbage?

———————

Betty is known as our first lady of the desert—and Jerry is known as the last man out of the sand trap.

Ford was the first president to use a lethal weapon . . . a golf club.

His wife founded the Betty Ford Center, which can cure anything except Jerry's slice.

I love playing golf with Gerald Ford. He makes me feel like I'm back performing in a war zone.

Actually, we get along well on the golf course. I never remind him that he used to be the president and he never reminds me that I used to be funny.

———————

BUT NOW CARTER **was the man in the Oval Office. He had the headaches.**

———————

Mr. Carter spent thirty years growing peanuts, and now he's got a whole Congress that sticks to the roof of his mouth.

CARTER WAS A CHURCHGOING peanut farmer from Plains, Georgia, who had a brother who brewed his own beer, an outspoken mother named Miss Lillian, and a southern accent so heavy that a special dictionary was published to help people understand him. All of these elements, plus an infectious smile, worked to his advantage.

———

It's official. Jimmy Carter has changed his address from Plains, Georgia, to "Down the road a piece."

Did you see the size of that crowd at the Inaugural Parade? Jimmy said, "Y'all come," and they did.

The swearing-in ceremony was out in the open. The Democrats applauded Jimmy Carter. The Republicans applauded the pigeons.

The Inaugural Ball had a Southern flavor. It was the first time "Hail to the Chief" was played on a jug and washboard.

Spring came to Washington, D.C. It's official. President Carter took off his sweater.

Mr. Carter is the first president we've had who considers a three-piece suit a sweater and two elbow patches.

He got calls on his radio talk show from people who never get to talk to the president—like kids, the poor, and the vice president.

Teddy Roosevelt asked us to "speak softly and carry a big stick." And it was John Kennedy who said, "Ask not what your country can do for you, but what you can do for your country." Now we have a president who says, "Y'all call collect, y'hear?"

The talk radio show was so successful, Carter decided to become the first president ever to be listed in the Yellow Pages.

Billy Carter tried to call in, but it's pretty hard to reach the White House from Plains, Georgia, just talking through a beer can and a string.

———————

IN 1976 I WAS asked to entertain at a White House dinner honoring Queen Elizabeth and her husband, Prince Philip. It was a night to remember. Whoever thought we'd be honored by the presence of the *real* King family!

———————

The Queen has a great sense of humor, which is one reason she came to Washington. If you want laughs, *this* is the place to *get* 'em!

What dignitaries are here tonight! Peter Lawford is parking the cars . . . and the peanut vendor's Jimmy Carter.

I've never seen so much royalty. This looks like a chess game . . . live.

There was so much blue blood, my fountain pen kept giving mating calls.

We just don't understand royalty in our country. Anytime we see a crown, we expect a margarine commercial.

The nearest thing we have to the monarchy are our president and vice president. But they have to run every four years, so *they* do the bowing.

DESPITE BRIGHT MOMENTS like those with the Queen, President Carter had lots of important issues to deal with, such as the Panama Canal and the Middle East. The country had nothing but praise and hope for the 1978 Camp David Accords, which were brokered by the president, but troubles remain to this day.

All I know about the canal is, it runs between Panama City and Colón . . . The cities that gave us straw hats and Preparation H.

Of course, the president is in favor of the treaty. With the luck we've been having lately . . . I think he wants to give the canal back before it springs a leak.

I hear Carter's plan is to give up the canal . . . then send Burt Lance down there to borrow it back.

In Washington, everyone's arguing over the Panama Canal. President Carter wants Congress to jump in.

Reagan not only wants to keep the canal, he'd like to open it as a swimming pool for underprivileged Democrats.

In the 1900s American know-how built the canal and swept Panama free of mosquitoes. Ronnie says, "Fair is fair. Let's keep the canal and give 'em back their mosquitoes."

Jimmy did so well at Camp David that now he's thinking about sending Congress to camp.

When the polls came out showing Carter's popularity had risen 11 percent, everyone went wild in the White House. They say Gatorade flowed like water.

I don't know why the Arabs are so mad at Carter. Is it his fault he suddenly had a craving for knishes?

They've given Sadat the highest penalty you can give an Arab citizen. They've banned him from the January white sales.

It's really something. Just think, the Israelis and the Arabs may finally bury the hatchet . . . when up to now, they haven't even been able to decide who owns the hatchet.

But it was a history-making meeting, and before Sadat left, they took him to the Wailing Wall for fifteen minutes of bipartisan wailing.

A lot of the Arabs are upset with Sadat. He has to be careful every morning now when he starts his camel.

When he stepped off the plane he received the highest Jewish welcome . . . "First we'll eat, then we'll talk."

And how about Anwar Sadat? What a history-making visit. Sadat being welcomed into Israel. That's like Billy Carter being welcomed into the White House.

———————

CARTER WAS ALSO ABLE to strike a trade agreement with China. Since China was opening up, I thought it would be a kick to be the first variety show from the West let into that previously

oppressive regime. I decided it was time to do a show in Beijing.

———————

It's a master stroke of diplomacy. Under the new alignment China and the United States become friends. And even Taiwan isn't left out . . . Taiwan gets Cleveland.

Trade's already commenced between the two countries. The Chinese are crazy about thousand-year-old eggs . . . so they just buy fresh eggs over here and have our post office deliver them.

In honor of the new Chinese treaty, the tree in the White House is decorated with tinsel and egg roll.

And I hear the president is thinking of getting rid of all his advisors. He's going to depend entirely on fortune cookies.

And beginning in March, we'll even have a Chinese embassy in Washington. They sent Mr. Carter a list of Chinese diplomats and he picked one from column "A" and two from column "B."

I'm leaving for China in a couple of weeks. Our State Department wasn't too happy about issuing the visa . . . I asked for a round trip.

The Chinese were gracious enough to invite me over. I hear I'm the *fifth* thing they're gonna modernize.

I really can't believe I'm here, but this must be China. Last night, I went to a movie called *The America Syndrome*. It's part of a cultural exchange . . . the State Department sends me over here and the Chinese send back a yak who can count to ten.

They even had a picture of me in the Peking paper. The caption said, "Our great beloved leaders invite important American tourist."

We had a great flight over, but I'll tell you one thing . . . this is a long way to come for a Coca-Cola.

And they gave me quite a ride to the hotel from the airport . . . twice I fell off the handlebars.

In China I've never seen such crowded streets, but they have it well organized. Slow traffic is on the bottom layer. All the Americans here are watching those bicycles very closely. If the gas shortage keeps up, by the time we get home they may be riding one.

And crossing the street here is like playing baseball in Los Angeles. You're either a Dodger or an Angel.

This is the only city I've been to where you can call a cab to go to a restaurant and the cabbie takes you right to the table. And can you believe the horns? Peking sounds like a whole city that just got married.

I said to the cabbie, "Why do you keep blowing your horn?" He said, "I can't hear you . . . I'm blowing my horn."

THINGS WERE NOT GOING too well for President Carter. There was a recession, inflation and unemployment were up, and the dollar was down. Carter said the problems could be solved, and there was no doubt that Jimmy tried his best to solve them—but they were too much. Carter left office as he entered it, a gentleman with a bodacious smile.

By the time election year 1980 came around, everyone was fair game.

———————

Among Republicans, Reagan is out in front, although no other prominent Republican has endorsed him. That figures—they're all running.

Reagan's defeat by George Bush in the Iowa primary is very biblical. It's only the second time in history someone received a message from a bush.

Ted Kennedy is appearing on TV every chance he gets. The other night he was pin boy on *Bowling for Dollars*.

Carter decided to start campaigning when he called his election headquarters and Joan Kennedy answered the phone. However, Billy helped—he didn't say anything.

Jerry Brown returned to Sacramento to find out that while he was campaigning [Lieutenant Governor] Mike Curb appointed another governor.

John Anderson decided to run as an Independent and has already suggested how to choose the winner. He wants to do it alphabetically.

The ballot narrowed down to Reagan and Bush versus Carter and Mondale. I referred to the debates as "The Jimmy and Ronnie Show," also known as "Championship Sniping." It was quite an event: Ultra Brite versus Brylcreem.

Reagan has been rehearsing for the inaugural all week. He wanted to do it in one take. Nancy had some trouble with him in rehearsing their first dance for the ball. It's not easy to follow a partner who keeps circling to the right.

The first day in office Reagan added some color and taste to the Oval Office—a jar full of jelly beans to offer his guests. Somehow I expected more of a change than from peanuts to jelly beans.

———

I HAD A LOT of fun with Ronnie. He and I had been friends since World War II days. It was great having an actor in the White House. It may have been his charm and general likability that prompted Pat Schroeder, a Democratic congresswoman from Colorado, to label the Reagan presidency as the "Teflon presidency"—no matter what went wrong, nothing seemed to stick to him. But for me the hallmark of the Reagan presidency was humor. The Reagans laughed at themselves. It was President Reagan who set the tone of humor after his assassination attempt. Upon entering the hospital, he wanted to know if the doctors were Republicans.

When Nancy was asked her opinion of Red China, she answered, "It's terrible, just terrible. It will clash with the drapes in the White House dining room."

Reagan's the only president I know who's going to have an opening act for the State of the Union Address.

But seriously, I think we should treat all of our presidents like stars . . . if their ratings are low, we should be able to cancel them.

I hear he's making himself at home. He spent his first day in the Rose Garden tearing out peanut vines and replacing them with jelly bean plants.

The first morning Mr. Reagan woke up in the White House, he forgot where he was and began clearing brush from the driveway.

Can you believe we have an actor in the White House? And Nancy Reagan is no longer the First Lady . . . now she's the leading lady.

And George Bush is no longer called the vice president . . . now he's called the understudy.

And Reagan's changing "Hail to the Chief" to "You Oughta Be in Pictures."

———————

THE MIDDLE EAST continued to be a powder keg. Beautiful Beirut, often called "the Paris of the Middle East," had become a war zone. Knowing that our military was over there made it easy to decide to do yet another overseas Christmas show.

Once again, I gathered together a troupe of eager entertainers.

Here we are on the hangar deck of the USS *Guam*, and I know why they call it the *Guam* . . . they just took the island and stuck a superstructure on it.

But I wanna tell you, we are in a part of the world where Santa uses a tail gunner on his sleigh.

Yes, sir. We're anchored right off the coast of Beirut . . . better known as Dodge City.

And may I tell you, it's been a while since I've entertained servicemen. But Washington told me, "If we can bring ships out of mothballs, why not you."

We've kept our travel arrangements pretty secret. The State Department said, "We want to keep your travels secret." I said, "So the enemy can't find me?" They said, "Yeah, them too."

They said, "We can't tell you where you're going, how long it will take, or when you'll get there." I love it when they treat me just like an enlisted man.

And I didn't get much sleep on the plane over here. I was traveling with Brooke Shields, Cathy Lee Crosby, Ann Jillian, Miss USA. Sleep? Hell, I didn't even get to blink. No, with treats like that, you don't want to miss anything.

We came in here on a wing and a prayer. I had the wing. That's because all the girls on board told me I didn't have a prayer.

THE PRESIDENTIAL CAMPAIGN of 1984 was between Ronald Reagan and Walter Mondale. Ronnie and George Bush won the election easily, which is something of an understatement. Mondale and his veep candidate, Geraldine Ferraro, carried only one state, Minnesota. Ronnie would have carried that one, too, but nobody told him it was there.

Hey, what a victory for the Reagans . . . or, as they're now being referred to . . . "Dynasty."

I wonder if anyone woke up the president and told him?

The Republicans fought hard . . . Their slogan was *"Don't fire until you see the bags under his eyes."*

I guess a lot of people just didn't want to see the country on the Fritz.

Mondale knew this was gonna be a bad day when he called *Dial-A-Prayer* and the taped message answered him by name.

Remember? Mondale said God has no place in politics, and apparently God feels the same way about Mondale.

Hey, did you hear the real reason Reagan wanted to be reelected? He needs four more years to finish that closing statement from the first debate.

George Bush decided to sleep late this morning . . .
he left a wake-up call for 1988.

I always get confused voting in California. There
are more propositions on the ballot than on the
Sunset Strip.

The campaigns go on so long now . . . the babies they
kissed when it started are now old enough to vote.

They were crisscrossing the country for so long, last
week, George Bush realized he'd kissed the same
baby three times.

They've kissed so many babies, their lips have
diaper rash.

The farmers hate to see it end. All those campaign
speeches were good for the crops.

Only in America would people spend millions of
dollars for a job that pays two hundred thousand
dollars a year. That's what the president makes.
Dave Winfield plays outfield for the Yankees and he
gets a million and a half a year . . . and he doesn't
have to jump over Tip O'Neill to get to first base.

I don't know if Jerry Falwell had anything to do with the landslide . . . but he carries a one-way walkie-talkie.

This morning he had his entire congregation ask God to "Win one for the Gipper." Somebody should tell Jerry Falwell that God is an Independent . . . he's not rich enough to be a Republican.

And Reagan wants to bring more religion into politics. He doesn't want to be sworn in with just a Bible . . . he wants to put his hand on the Tablets with the Ten Commandments . . . He's already called Charlton Heston and asked if he could borrow them.

———————

Reagan topped all my jokes that year with one of his own. Testing the microphone for his weekly radio broadcast, he said, "My fellow Americans, I'm pleased to tell you today that I've signed legislation that will outlaw Russia forever. We begin bombing in five minutes."

Somehow the joke got on the air. If it had been Orson Welles who said it, it would have caused a national panic. But since it was Reagan, nobody took it seriously. They just figured Nancy had forgotten to make out his cue cards.

One of the country's main distractions, once the elections were over, was another competition—the Olympics. In 1984, they were held in my backyard, Los Angeles.

———————

Didn't you love the Olympics? . . . or as the USA Team calls them, "The California Gold Rush of '84."

The Olympic spirit is still in the air in Los Angeles . . . I think it's stuck between the smog and the ozone layer.

And it's no wonder there wasn't any smog in Los Angeles for the Olympics. There was so much flag-waving, they fanned it out to sea.

But, thank God there wasn't a smog problem! As many times as the band played "Oh, say, can you see," it would have been embarrassing to hear all the athletes answer, "No!"

Those games took me to the height of patriotism; they made me almost glad to be a taxpayer.

The patriotism welled up inside me. I know it was patriotism, because at my age when anything wells up inside me, I have the doctor check it out.

Everybody was a true American for the Olympics. During those two weeks, Henry Kissinger spoke without an accent.

Howard Cosell stuck his tongue out at a referee and it was red, white, and blue.

Our people kept cheering for anything that was red, white, and blue. I saw a group of them on the street corner screaming for a mailbox to go faster.

Wasn't it something? I had my hand over my heart so often the alligator on my breast pocket started chewing my nails.

People are once again singing along with the national anthem, instead of betting whether the vocalist will hit the high note or not.

I met a guy the other day who had watched every single Olympic event on television . . . I know because he had five circles under each eye!

And Reagan was made an honorary team member, and he qualified . . . He may never have been in a relay race, but as a politician he knows how to pass the buck.

And now I hear there's even a movement to put Carl Lewis on Mount Rushmore.

The first line of "America" now goes "My country, 'tis of thee . . . sweet land of Mary Lou Retton."

But I think it's great and we've sure come a long way from the sixties, haven't we? It's so much nicer to see kids burning an Olympic Torch than a draft card.

ONE OF THE more interesting characters to come on the world political stage was Mikhail Gorbachev. He was a colorful guy and a great target for some of my lampoons.

Did you hear that Gorbachev is insisting that dissenting opinions be allowed? So from now on, Raisa will let him say whatever he wants around the house.

There are so many problems facing Gorbachev, he's thinking of going someplace where he'd be appreciated. I hear he might run for mayor of Washington.

There's bad news and good news for the Soviet leader. The bad news is, his country is falling apart. The good news is, he didn't have any money in Lincoln Savings & Loan.

If you criticize Gorbachev too much, you're kaputski. Kaputski . . . it's an Old Russian word meaning, "Siberia is lovely this time of year."

This isn't the first time they've had freedom of speech in Russia . . . but it's the first time people may still be around to use it a second time.

You can tell the Russians are feeling much friendlier toward the United States. Their spies have been told to stop trying to break our Zip Code.

One reason the Communist party is losing out is because people would rather be fed than red.

One Communist asked another, "What do they mean by a free election?" The other one said, "That means you're free to vote any way they tell you to."

Nancy Reagan's not too thrilled about all this. She thought red was going to be in fashion for a few more years.

The Russian people might have a tough time making a choice. I understand they're still having trouble deciding between Big Macs and Quarter-Pounders.

But most of the Russian people are behind the change. In fact, "KGB" now stands for "Kiss Gorby, Baby."

But can you believe all that is happening in the world today? I haven't seen this many changes take place before my eyes since I thumbed through Michael Jackson's old photo albums.

You can hear two things in Moscow today: people singing "Happy Days Are Here Again" and the sound of Lenin spinning in his grave.

CHRISTMAS CAME A LITTLE early for me. You can imagine how excited I was when I learned that President Reagan decided to honor me as an *actor* with the Kennedy Center Honors. The others selected for the '85 medals were opera singer Beverly Sills; dancer Merce Cunningham; composers Lerner and Loewe; and actress Irene Dunne.

I can't tell you what a thrill it is to be invited to the State Department to receive the Kennedy Center Honors. It was the first time security ever let in a comedian who wasn't in Congress.

But this is something for a former vaudevillian . . . to be able to come to Washington because of fast footwork on stage, instead of the political arena.

Sitting among such distinguished honorees, it finally dawned on me how they may have been chosen. They never made a movie with me.

But I did have a little problem at the door. They figured I was a gate crasher and I thought I was being arrested when Ed Meese jumped up and started reading me my rights.

I enjoy coming to Washington to get an award. I love to get anything here that's not taxable.

It's great for a comedian to be honored in Washington. If there was ever a city that knew how to get laughs.

This is a real thrill . . . to get an award from Washington and I don't even know who I'm supposed to vote for yet.

There are so many congressmen and senators here, I don't know whether to tell a joke or pass a bill . . . as if there was a difference.

Congress may be going home for the holidays soon. How can you beat a Christmas gift like that?

―――――

ONE OF THE truly amazing things I saw in the '80s was Halley's Comet. At eighty-two, I'd already seen it once before, but at six I had other kinds of stars in my eyes. Dolores bought me a telescope, which I set up in Palm Springs. Boy, can you see the stars down there, and I don't mean the two-legged kind. The desert nights are beautiful, and that comet was something else.

Say, Halley's Comet is coming around again. I didn't know what all the excitement's about. I've seen it so many times, I'm getting dizzy!

And how about Halley's Comet arriving after seventy-six years? There hasn't been this much excitement over a ball of fire since Tip O'Neill accidentally backed into his barbecue pit.

Yeah, it comes by every seventy-six years. It keeps the same schedule as my fan club.

They say it'll be visible until April . . . except, of course, for two weeks in February when it goes behind Tip O'Neill.

That's right. It's going to be visible until tax time. The same thing could be said about my money.

Imagine. Every seventy-six years . . . In Los Angeles, the sky only appears that often.

I was in school the last time Halley's Comet appeared and I remember a test we had. It said, "A comet is a star with a tail. Name a famous one." I wrote down, "Rin Tin Tin."

No, it last came around in 1909 and then disappeared. I wonder if it was something we said.

Seventy-six years between visits. I can't wait to see if it looks the same as it did the first time I saw it.

It takes Halley's Comet seventy-six years to get here. Big deal, so does a home-delivered pizza.

———————

DURING MY TRAVELS, I had a chance to spend some time in the Philippines. It's a great country with some beautiful resort areas. The people are warm and friendly—and then there's Ferdinand Marcos.

———————

They say Marcos has eight billion dollars. That's not bad for a guy who's too short to play basketball.

And how about all the land they've discovered Ferdinand Marcos owns? Isn't that something? Now we find out Marcos owns half of America . . . and he's not even Japanese.

That Philippine election is really something, isn't it? I won't say it's rigged, but surveys show that four out of every two people voted for Marcos.

They suspect it may have been a crooked election. So far, one candidate has seventy-eight percent of the votes, and the other one has seventy-three percent of the votes . . . and that's with only three percent of the island reporting.

President Reagan sent Senator Lugar to Manila as an observer. After he got back, he told the president, "I didn't see anything suspicious when I voted."

The team of U.S. observers saw so much cheating, they thought they accidentally got off the plane in Chicago.

It was an historic election anyway. It's the first time any country has ever used a ballot box that flushes.

Let's face it; February wasn't a good month for presidents. One lost his country, another could lose an election, and Reagan's youngest son lost his pants.

Ronald Reagan called Marcos when he went through Honolulu, even though he was mad at him. He found out that Marcos owns his ranch in Santa Barbara.

Here we are at Clark Air Base . . . from the Philippine language meaning: "Who's got the key?"

A weather forecast here is humidity followed by sweating and fainting.

It gets so humid here, I'm wearing special makeup. It's half coolant.

I noticed quite a few natives going barefoot. Did Imelda Marcos take all the shoes with her?

———————

A T CHRISTMASTIME IN 1987, I made a trip to the Persian Gulf, along with Barbara Eden, Lee Greenwood, Connie Stevens, and her daughters.

We moved from ship to ship with a few stops to restock the Dramamine. The guys, as always, were happy to see the gals and me . . . well, I had a few jokes for them.

We did our first show aboard ship. Besides hearing jokes about life on base or aboard ship, the audience always loves to hear the latest on the home front.

We're on the way to the Persian Gulf. It's a mistake! I thought they said Persian Golf.

I don't believe in escorting tankers that are taking Oil of Olay to Tammy Bakker.

We shouldn't pick on her. She's having a terrible time now . . . she's in the Betty Ford Center, suffering from terminal mascara abuse. Just when she's starting her new church: Our Lady of Avon.

Merry Christmas! Here we are in the Persian Gulf aboard the *Okinawa* based in Yokosuka. How do you say that? Yokosuka. I said that three times fast in rehearsal and my tongue just got out of traction.

I'm glad the *Okinawa* had experience as the prime recovery ship for *Apollo 8* and *15*. One of your men kissed Barbara Eden earlier, so you can recover him when he comes down to earth . . .
It's the only time sailors will be paid for making a pickup.

The crew works at staying in shape . . . some guys run or lift weights. I saw one sailor trying to bench-press a dinner roll.

This is a big ship. I'm sorry now I didn't pack my golf cart.

I did take a walk around the ship. I had to sprinkle bread crumbs to find my way back to my quarters.

And I have to tell you guys, I'm having a little trouble getting used to all the Navy terms you use. I keep hearing the word "bilge." What's bilge? Okay, I get the idea. You don't have to keep pointing at the cue cards.

And what an exciting fall we've been having on TV, right? It had mystery, intrigue, suspense, lying, cheating, extramarital sex . . . but enough about the presidential race.

I don't know if the presidential candidates are running for the White House or Animal House.

The Hart scandal changes everything. Voters won't know what to think when they hear a candidate has changed positions.

You remember when a politician "pressed the flesh" it just meant he was shaking hands?

And how about evangelist Pat Robertson? He's already tossed his halo in the ring . . . He had his first child eight weeks after he was married . . . That's the kinda guy we need in there . . . a guy who gets it done fast . . . Poor Pat. Before he said, "I do," he did.

I don't know if Jesse Jackson is trying to appeal to a broader audience, but I just saw him doing a commercial for Wonder Bread.

As you all know, Gary Hart threw his hat in the ring again. I guess he finally remembered where he left it.

Gary Hart's back in the race for ten minutes and already he's the front-runner. If I follow that logic, God help us if Jim Bakker decides to run.

Gary Hart said, "I have no money and no staff, but I do have ideas." Getting ideas was what got him in trouble in the first place.

ONCE AGAIN, THE PRESIDENTIAL PRIMARIES were under way. On a personal note, I hated to see the Reagans leave the White House. Ronnie provided lots of good material—I think I have more Reagan jokes in my files than for any other president.

President Reagan hated making budget cuts, but he had no choice. He got all choked up when he had to tell Lee Iacocca, "Sorry, no more food stamps."

And to set an example, he's been making sacrifices, too. Did you know he's now buying day-old jelly beans?

And some of his Reaganomics took real courage. Like when he said to Nancy, "I hate to tell you this, but we're going to have to make do with the same old tablecloths."

Budget Director David Stockton blabbed that Reagan's economic program was designed to help the rich. Well, if the Republicans won't help them, who will?

Secretary of State Alexander Haig, Secretary of Defense Caspar Weinberger, and National Security Advisor Richard Allen are all feuding. At Cabinet breakfasts all they put out are plastic knives.

Did you see that President Reagan finally got a hearing aid? People have been telling Reagan to get one for years—but he couldn't hear them.

He only wears it in his right ear because he doesn't want to hear from the left.

I knew he was having trouble hearing when he was looking at his watch and I asked him, "What time is it?" And he answered, "Bulova."

Actually, it was Congress who talked him into getting it. They've been telling him to stick it in his ear for years.

I N 1988, IT WAS "open season" on all the voters again. But it boiled down to Massachusetts governor Michael Dukakis and Lloyd Bentsen of Texas challenging Vice President George Bush and Dan Quayle.

It was no surprise to anyone that I jumped on the Bush bandwagon early in the game. George and Barbara Bush were like family. I knew his father, Prescott, and played golf with him. During his eight years as Reagan's vice president, I became very close to George and I played a lot of golf with him too. Bush and Quayle easily won the election and Bush got off to a good start.

George was brought up to be a politician. Before he learned how to crawl, he already knew how to shake hands.

At age two, George said his first words: "How am I doing in the polls?"

When Dukakis was a boy, he lived in a poor neighborhood. When George was a boy, his father showed him a picture of one.

George Bush will soon be sworn in, but I still have to come to grips with whether he'll repeat the oath or we'll have to read his lips.

You know, George Bush had an image problem: before the convention, people thought he was such a wimp, the polo player on his shirt rode sidesaddle . . . I said to Bush, "It's a miracle that you're so much better than you were before." He said, "I think the same thing about you, whenever you're funny."

Bush and Quayle have been sworn in, and the country will do just fine. But I still can't picture Reagan in an unemployment line.

Did you know that George Bush, our new president, is a fisherman, a hunter, plays tennis, and at Yale, played baseball and football? He's so sports-minded that after the inauguration yesterday, when he swore on the Bible, he went inside and swore again on the *Sporting News*. Talk about being an athlete. Bush will be the first president to greet foreign leaders with a high five.

Did you see all the Bush kids and grandkids at the inauguration? They may turn the White House into a day-care center. Did you see the picture of President Bush reading a fairy tale to his grandchildren? I think it was called the Federal Budget.

Bush is in Colombia this week for a summit meeting with all the world leaders. It's a scary situation down there. They began the summit with a prayer. It lasted for five hours.

The *L.A. Times* gave George Bush a "C" on his first one hundred days in office. No one knows what Dan Quayle got. He claims he lost his report card on his way home from the White House.

The president was criticized for not responding soon enough to the *Exxon Valdez* crisis. I don't know. I think his idea of using five million Q-tips wasn't bad.

The president is real serious about reducing air pollution. He wants to clean up our air by the year 2000. I just hope we can hold our breath until then.

Did you hear that the first dog, Millie, is writing her memoirs? I understand that one of the titles under consideration is *Read My Paws*. All this is according to her typist, Barbara Bush.

Did you read that the president is out of the country again? Now it can be told. George Bush never wanted the presidency—all he wanted were the frequent flyer miles.

Did you see President Bush golfing this past week? He likes to play once in a while. It gives him a chance to swear at something other than Congress.

George Bush went for eighteen days on his vacation without catching a fish. I didn't know that many bass were Democrats.

George Bush is declaring war on drugs. Let's hope he has more luck catching the drug dealers than he has had catching fish.

As you know, horseshoes is a favorite game of the Bush family. However, I think the president has an uphill battle in trying to make the sport our national pastime.

I hear that Santa is going to bring something to President Bush that he's had trouble getting all year—a fish. Santa made an early visit to the White House. All eleven Bush grandkids were there, and there was a lot of pushing and shoving to see who could talk to Santa first. Finally, Barbara Bush stepped in and told Dan Quayle that he would have to wait his turn.

———

FOR THE MOST PART, President Bush received good grades for his management of foreign affairs. The Berlin Wall came down and the Soviet Union and Eastern Europe were testing democracy. I was very interested to see the end of the Berlin Wall. I had experienced it during the Berlin Airlift, and I wanted to be sure it was really being torn down. I did a show for our troops stationed at Tempelhof Air Base in Germany.

———

In my lifetime, I saw that Berlin Wall come and I saw it go. It used to be if you tried to cross this wall, you could be shot at. In Los Angeles, that happens if you try to change lanes on the freeway.

I did buy a piece of the wall the other day, but I think I was taken. On the back it was stamped, "Made in Japan."

How about what's happening in Germany, though. The East Germans are still coming into West Germany. So many are here now, the country's beginning to tilt. Just yesterday 353 Germans fell into France.

And a lot of people came West who didn't even want to come. They thought that the long line was people waiting to get in to see *The Teenage Mutant Ninja Turtles.*

But you know, this Berlin . . . it's amazing. They're turning away from Communism so they can be more like us. Isn't it great to know that we're a winner? Especially when we're three trillion dollars in the hole.

I N THE FALL of 1990, all hell broke loose on the international front when Saddam Hussein decided to annex Kuwait. Once again, our men and women in uniform were being called upon to serve, and I wanted to spend Christmas with them—which is what I did. Dolores insisted on going with me. She loved singing to all the guys, and they sure loved her.

———————

I'm glad to be here with you. I wasn't crazy about the invitation, though. Your C.O. said, "Bob, the guys want to have their turkey on Christmas, so don't be late."

Anyway, I gotta tell you, this is Bob "with Operation Desert Shield . . . somewhere in Saudi Arabia" Hope.

I asked the general what I could do to be really popular with you guys. He said, "Dress up as the mailman."

You know, the only thing over here that would be more popular than mail is female . . . I'll tell you that a lot of people are writing to soldiers they don't even know. One guy gets thirty letters a week from Ed McMahon.

One infantryman couldn't figure out why his brother sent him a toy balloon . . . until he blew it up and it turned out to be an inflatable woman . . . Now he thinks he's falling in love . . . In the meantime, he found out there's such a thing as sub-leasing an inflatable woman.

And the guys invited me this afternoon to see their tents. You fellas have done amazing things to your tents . . . considering you don't drink.

And I asked a soldier what he'd most like to hang in his tent. He said, "Saddam Hussein."

One soldier told me he misses his girlfriend, but the first thing he's going to do when he gets home is take a shower. I said, "What's the first thing you're going to do alone?"

You know we've come a hell of a long way to find you guys from Twenty-nine Palms. I've seen you staggering around in Palm Springs on Saturday nights and I wish to hell you were going home with me.

I asked a Marine corporal if the troops enjoyed President Bush's visit last Thanksgiving. And he said, "Not nearly as much as the troops would've enjoyed visiting President Bush."

The Saudis were afraid Iraq was already using poison gas, then they found out it was American GI cooking odors blowing in.

I just don't get the Arabs in the Middle East. Who'd think men who could have as many wives as they want would have the energy to go to war, huh?

These guys are tough, these Marines. They use barbed wire for dental floss.

Their motto is Semper Fidelis . . . which means Mike Tyson is a sissy.

President Bush did everything he said he was going to do. It's a whole new concept in politics. His popularity is so high now that he can leave politics and become a rock star.

———————

NOBODY KNOWS WHAT HAPPENED in the 1992 presidential race. Bush's popularity ratings were high, he had all his ducks in a row—and one Quayle—but it wasn't to be. The major issues of that election year were the struggling national economy, health care, and Ross Perot's haircut.

William Jefferson Clinton had an infectious smile, à la Franklin Roosevelt, the charm of Jimmy Carter, and Ronald Reagan's ability to romance an audience, be it in person or on television.

———————

Well, the election campaign in the country is picking up speed. The voters are yawning faster. All the candidates are talking about health care now. Don't they realize that it's their campaign speeches that make us sick? . . . You know, we could wipe out the federal deficit if there was a tax on campaign promises.

All the candidates are coming to California. Clinton is trying to convince Californians that he's one of them. Yesterday, he held a press conference while hangin' ten in the surf off Malibu.

Having a saxophone player in the White House could be interesting. Clinton may not pull us out of the recession, but while the country is singing the blues, he can play along.

Now that Clinton has made an elephant disappear, maybe he can do the same thing with the deficit.

It's a different type of Christmas in Washington this year. You can tell there's a Christmas on Capitol Hill. The Nativity scene is on the lawn in front of Congress, and the three wise men all have Arkansas accents.

And the way Bill Clinton plays the saxophone, he's not selecting a Cabinet, he's looking for sidemen. Leave it to a politician to be good at playing a wind instrument. He may have the first Cabinet in history with a rhythm section.

Bill Clinton has spent a lot of time jogging around Washington. I'm not saying he doesn't look too good in his jogging shorts, but the Lincoln statue has its hands over its eyes.

Y'know, the Clintons may have to take a bus to the inauguration. The Bush administration hasn't returned the presidential limo yet. Bill Clinton taking a bus to the inauguration isn't bad. The alternative is his driving a tractor.

Clinton loves to make long speeches. In fact, this will be the first inaugural address with an intermission.

The Clintons will have an open house. That means anyone can get in, even Republicans. The Clintons wanted to invite the public into their new home, but Hillary said, "They can come in, but I'm not going to bake anything for them."

I'm a little suspicious of the invitation. I think they just wanted us to help them unpack.

DOLORES AND I like to call this decade "The Back Nine," an old golfing term. It's been an amazing life, looking back. I guess you could say that I have been driven by the sound of laughter. All that good energy in the air. Someone once pointed out that the human being is the only being on the planet that has the ability to laugh. I guess that's why I always found my best audience to be humans.

It's a time for me to look back and enjoy. Life has slowed down a bit for both Dolores and me, or at least it feels like it. We still enjoy our homes in the desert and on Toluca Lake. We love our golf, our dogs, and our family; in fact, I was just introduced to my thirty-something grandchildren, Zachary, Andrew, and Miranda. Amazing what you miss when you're on the run. And most of all, I'm getting a chance to spend time with Dolores. At least I think it's Dolores—she looks familiar.

The first of May, Dolores and I started rehearsing our act to be performed aboard the *QE2* as part of a D day commemoration recognizing the fiftieth anniversary of the invasion. The *QE2* had booked a whole ship full of World War II veterans and their families, who were returning to Normandy. What an audience! And the ship!

All this luxury on a cruise ship is important to some people, but not me. I'm just glad it floats.

And this ship is just as elegant as any hotel. The only drawback is that the doorman can't call you a cab.

I usually don't do this much walking . . . unless there's a golf ball involved.

Is this a ship or one of Ross Perot's bath toys?

And the food on board is elegant. Of course, when you're in the middle of the ocean, everything is imported.

I am proud to introduce Dolores. Behind every successful man there's a woman . . . telling him to keep moving . . . or else!

Dolores and I consider this cruise our second honeymoon. In fact, after sixty years we forgot whether we ever had a first one or not.

But I'm just as romantic today as I was when we were first married. Either that or my Dramamine is starting to wear off.

She still laughs at my jokes. Come to think of it, she laughs at a lot of things I do lately.

———

ON MEMORIAL DAY, we flew into New York City to take the Concorde to England. We arrived in England (four hours earlier than our stomachs) and checked into the Savoy for a day of rest and to work on some new "back home in England" material for our *QE2* shows. We had scheduled a few performances at the Royal Albert Hall in London and in Glasgow, Scotland, once the cruise was over. I couldn't let good material go to waste.

———

Boy, the Concorde travels fast. It's like being shot out of a cannon—first class.

It's so fast that they don't have time to lose your luggage.

If you want to take a nap on the flight, you have to fall asleep during pre-boarding.

In the flight magazine the crossword puzzle only has four words.

They don't have in-flight movies. They just show coming attractions.

Instead of a bathroom on board, they just have a sign that says, "We won't be that long. Hold it."

I was born in England . . . no matter how hard England tries to tell you differently.

England sent me to America when I was four years old. It was their way of getting even for the Revolutionary War.

I was born in a town called Eltham. That was a long time ago . . . and the town hasn't lived it down yet.

England is my native country. Of course, I don't speak the language anymore.

True, I have trouble with the language in England. Someone called with a teatime the other day. I thought he meant golf . . . I was the only one there stirring my tea with a seven-iron.

My relatives always greet me at the airport with a big banner. It says "Yankee Go Home."

I DECLARED MYSELF a "free agent" with my final NBC television special in November 1996. Fittingly, it was called "Laughing with the Presidents," a recap of my relationships with them from Franklin on . . . No, not Benjamin Franklin, Franklin Roosevelt. The whole thing was pretty nostalgic for me.

I've enjoyed sixty remarkable years with NBC. Sixty years . . . I started before the peacock and he wound up taking my parking place.

I've been with NBC so long. I was here when the peacock was just an egg . . . in fact, I may have laid it.

A lot has changed. When they used to do my face before a show, it was called makeup . . . now it's called special effects.

I've been with NBC for sixty years. Someday I've got to get a real job.

This is my sixtieth year on television with NBC, which proves that Abraham Lincoln was wrong—you can fool all of the people all the time.

As a free agent, I'll finally have time to do something I always wanted to do—travel.

THE YEAR 1997 was truly eventful for me. For my birthday, the U.S. Navy named a ship after me—the USNS *Bob Hope* (AKR 300)—requested by the Army, built by civilians and manned by the Navy, and named after a comedian. (Something there doesn't fit . . . nevertheless.) There was a great celebration at the Avondale Shipyards in New Orleans. Dolores christened the ship. I think she was planning to use holy water instead of champagne. (Dolores is very Catholic; I'm a comedian by religion.)

I think it is very fitting that I should have a ship named after me. I've spent most of my golfing life in the water.

And the timing couldn't have been better. This thing is going out to sea just when I'm ready to go into dry dock.

But this is always what I wanted to be . . . Bob Hope, star of stage, screen, and salt water.

One thing upsets me. They named this ship after me and it has a beam that measures 105 feet and 10 inches.

No, it's a beautiful ship. Put wheels on this and it'd make a terrific golf cart.

AND A COUPLE of trips to Washington, D.C., gave me a chance to polish up some of my political jokes—a subject matter I hadn't done in a while.

I like to come to Washington, D.C., at least once a year. Why should my tax money travel more than I do?

Washington, D.C., serves a very important function in our system of government. It keeps all the politicians in one place where it's easier to keep an eye on them.

It's a lot like summer camp. This is the place our politicians come to learn to sink or swim.

———————

AND JUST WHEN I started getting my sea legs, the U.S. Air Force named a C-17 Globemaster III *The Spirit of Bob Hope.* I've always marveled how a big ship can float—but for a piece of machinery like a C-17 to stay in the air is mind-boggling. I really wanted to take this baby home, but they didn't let me. I have to tell you I was so proud when I saw that "my plane" was the one that brought back the hostages captured in China a few years later.

Probably the most touching of all the honors I've ever received is the tribute Congress paid in 1998. Through the passage of Resolution 75, I was made an honorary veteran of the United States. The ceremony was held there in that beautiful Capitol building . . . It took me some time to recover in order to respond.

I've been given many awards in my lifetime, but to be numbered among the men and women I admire the most is the greatest honor I have ever received.

I was also caught off guard when I was informed in February 1998 that by order of Her Majesty Queen Elizabeth II, I was to receive an honorary knighthood—Knight Commander of the Most Excellent Order of the British Empire (KBE). At first I could only say, "I'm speechless! Seventy years of ad-lib material and I'm speechless." What an honor for a boy born in England, raised in Cleveland, and educated in vaudeville. If Mom could see me now.

And if that wasn't enough, the Pope got into the act. Dolores and I were accorded papal honors, Knight Commander and Dame of St. Gregory with star. I think they added the star part just for me.

For my ninety-fifth birthday, we had a western-themed party in the backyard complete with my favorite "In-'n'-Out" burgers. I was honored with a parade down Riverside Drive in Toluca Lake, my adopted hometown. A prebirthday surprise was having three hundred Vietnam POWs attend a special anniversary dinner at the Nixon Library and sing

"Happy Birthday" to me. Both Dolores and I did a little show. She sang and sounded so great. All I could come up with were jokes about getting older.

———————

My secret for staying young is good food, plenty of rest, and a makeup man with a spray gun.

My doctor says I've got everything going for me. Unfortunately, he can't stop any of it from going.

It feels great to be ninety-five. I mean, for those parts of me that still have feeling.

Age is only a number. However, in my case, it is a rather large number.

No, I do the same things I did when I was fifty-five. I just take a nap after each one now.

People are living longer nowadays, which is great. We finally found something that pleases both us and the insurance companies.

The best way to look young is to hang out with older people . . . For me, that's getting harder and harder to do.

AND THEN THERE WAS the opening of the Bob Hope Gallery of Entertainment at the Library of Congress in our nation's capital.

Earlier in the year I had given all my papers, videos, and films to the Library of Congress with the hopes that they would share my treasures with the American public. After all, they are really what the collection is all about. They have all my jokes, too. I figure years from now, new generations of Americans can visit the Library and take a walk through history and have a laugh or two.

My last years have been pretty quiet. Dolores and I enjoy our time together. She still beats me at gin rummy. I think I owe her $17,360, but she's willing to run a tab.

That writer who once said, "Bob, if you had your life to live over again, you wouldn't have time," may have had it right, but at almost one hundred I'd like to give it a try. It's been a hell of a ride.

ACKNOWLEDGMENTS

Bob Hope: My Life in Jokes includes material previously published in the following:

I Never Left Home, Bob Hope, 1944 (Simon & Schuster).

So This Is Peace, Bob Hope, 1946 (Simon & Schuster).

Have Tux, Will Travel, Bob Hope as told to Pete Martin, 1954 (Simon & Schuster).

Bob Hope: A Life in Comedy, William Robert Faith, 1982 (G.P. Putnam's Sons).

Don't Shoot, It's Only Me, Bob Hope with Melville Shavelson, 1990 (G.P. Putnam's Sons).

I Was There, Bob Hope, 1994 (Hope Enterprises, Inc.).

Dear Prez, I Wanna Tell Ya, a Presidential Jokebook, Bob Hope, edited by Ward Grant, 1996 (Hope Enterprises, Inc.).

SPECIAL THANKS FROM LINDA HOPE:

· To Ward Grant, for help with the last chapter, *I Was There,* and *Dear Prez.* For thirty-one years of spreading the word and for his constant encouragement.

- To Jan Morrill, keeper of the jokes and principal researcher for this book.

- To Marjorie Hughes, who kept such careful records for so many years . . . so many years ago.

- To Annette Siegel, for her help in keeping us all organized.

- To Jim Hardy, for his astonishing knowledge of the Bob Hope TV specials and video library.

- To Nancy Warnke, for her nimble fingers and good humor amid an avalanche of paper. Hopefully, she had a few laughs along the way.

- To Nancy Malone, who lent moral support and fed me during the big rush.

- Finally, to Marty Sklar, for coming up with the idea for this book in the first place and then for helping to make it happen.